THE HOPEFUL
BRAIN

NeuroTransactional Repair for Disconnected Children and Youth

Dr. Paul W. Baker and
Dr. Meredith White-McMahon

Contents

Introduction

Disconnected young people desperately need hope to be courageous in life. Despite living in a society that seems to cherish individuality, our young people are social and so they learn and grow best in the company of others. From the moment that people are born, everyone and everything in their ecology has a significant influence upon them. Our brains create ourselves in the context of these relationships and encounters. Without hope, our brains and bodies would constantly react, rather than respond to the ecologies around us in ways that are far from beneficial. We are our experiences. They shape who we are and who we will become.

How our brains develop in the context of our relationships impacts: how well we form attachments with others, how well we learn, and how we are affected by, and cope with, factors like success, challenge, isolation, mental illness, stress, and trauma. However, becoming the result of our relationships and experiences can be a double-edged sword. They can create healthy, functional individuals and healthy brain growth, or dysregulated, dysfunctional, and unhealthy individuals with far from optimal brain growth and development. The quality of a person's relational and ecological support is a significant contributor to healthy outcomes.

For decades, neuroscientists have known that through experience, the brain is changeable or neuroplastic in the early years of development. Over 50 years ago, neuroscientists realized that brain cells, or neurons, were able to change and modify their activity in response to environmental experiences. Neurons that fired together, wired together creating brain connections (Hebb, 1949). The problem was that neuroscientists also believed that after the critical period of those early years, the brain was no longer capable of change, leaving people with little hope. Based on these beliefs, most research and therapeutic efforts focused on early childhood. Because learning and behavior were believed to be entrenched by the teenage years there was little hope of change. This instilled a sense of "false permanence". Fortunately, new science is emerging across disciplines and shaping a more positive outlook of the individual's ability to change throughout the lifespan.

The advent of advanced neuroimaging technologies in the last 30 years has further shown that while natural developmental milestones and sensitive periods of enhanced neuroplasticity exist, new neurons continue to appear in parts of the brain related to new learning, and new neural networks appear and grow throughout life. Instead of our brains being the individual, isolated, self-organizing systems that neuroscientists assumed them to be, we now know that our brains are dependent on interactions with others and supportive ecologies for survival, growth, and well-being throughout our entire lifespan.

This is great news for anyone working with challenging young people. By being a part of their experiences, therapeutic helpers are able to activate and guide change within the brain, encouraging growth and development to facilitate new learning and better adaptation to the ecological systems in which the child lives. Our NeuroTransactional model, a strengths-based approach, recognizes the brain's unique willingness to make changes for the better. By blending essential elements of neuroscience within a relational framework, this model will show that, together with our challenging young people, you can create optimal experiences that can shape, reshape, and transform. By "being with, feeling with, and going with" these young people, you become the catalyst for positive change and a significant factor in shaping their social-emotional development. You will assist in the identification, facilitation, and the eventual reimbursement of necessary skills and experiences that will change the youth's brain for the better

CHAPTER 1

Hope and Opportunity

People don't come pre-assembled, but are glued together
by life.
Joseph LeDoux

A Model of Hope and Opportunity

In this book we will take a NeuroTransactional approach to the natural biological development and interpersonal repair of the broken lives of disconnected young people. In this approach, we strive to demonstrate that brains and bodies, when given positive relationships and experiences, have the ability to change negative life events into positive outcomes. We will endeavor to instill encouragement. There is tremendous hope for all young people, no matter where they have come from, the experiences that they have endured, or the approaches they have taken towards life. People can overcome adversity. Disconnected youth can become better connected to life when caring, NeuroTransactionally trained people are involved in their day-to-day events. This model will counter historical approaches that have addressed and labeled the tough to reach with negative words and phrases such as disordered, dysfunctional, "just like his father," oppositional, "bad," hopeless, sociopathic, and a host of other identifiers that might doom a child to a reputation to either "live up to" or to "turn around." For years many scientists and mental health practitioners have bought into the misconception that both "personality" and the human brain were fully formed and unchangeable by the time a person reached adolescence. However, we have seen the evidence, both in research and in the field, that indicates that there is tremendous hope for even the most challenging of youth. Evidence in neuroscience (the study of the brain) and various disciplines within the field of psychology (the study of the mind) now clearly shows that people possess far more potential than ever expected; we are no longer on a predetermined "timeline" for the development of our true human potential. To those of us providing direct care, who work with those young people who approach life differently, this is both exceptional news and a tremendous responsibility. We, as therapeutic helpers, can no longer "write off" a child because of their past experiences. We must now write a child "into" a transformed life, one filled with better people, experiences, ecologies, health, meaningful academics, and closer connections to his or her individual culture.

The NeuroTransactional Model

The NeuroTransactional Model is powerful, positive and strength-based. The primary purpose of this model is to provide a way for those of us working with children and youth to address and fulfill their needs by tapping into the power of relationships and harnessing the possibilities of an ever-changing brain with the hope of transforming lives. Relationships involve transactions that continually impact experience and development across the lifespan of everyone involved, and they can become a powerful opportunity for transformation. Everyone, even our most troubled children and youth, should be hopeful that they would thrive, not only as individuals but also as a part of a larger community. We see transformation as an integrative process. Focusing on the various biological, regulatory, relational, ecological, cultural, and academic needs that may be lacking or missing, therapeutic helpers and youth work together to understand how people and ecologies in their life can better meet those needs.

The NeuroTransactional Model provides comprehensive support by blending the best of relational practice with neuroscience. Understanding how the various systems within the brain function provides the foundational knowledge to increase the effectiveness and strength of the relationships. With that knowledge, we can better understand how to interact with others more efficiently and effectively. We believe that over time these interactions will encourage natural strengths to surface to help overcome adversity. This, in turn, will lead to personal motivation, more resilient skills, and, finally, transformation to successful coping.

The NeuroTransactional Model can be divided into two basic approaches: short-term or momentary management, and long-term therapeutic planning. You will learn more about the model's momentary management techniques in Chapter 2, ACT QUICK. Long-term therapeutic planning strategies are discussed in detail in Chapter 5.

NeuroTransactional Beliefs

One doesn't have to be professionally trained to be therapeutic to youth in need. The simple desire to help youth overcome their experiential challenges and actively participate in positive therapeutic planning and support is all that is needed! We believe that effective and optimistic agents of change hope for the best, try their best, and expect the best from all youth (and the therapeutic helper him/herself).

No matter what the history of the young person might encompass, there is a fund of what we term NeuroTransactional strategies that people can use with challenging young people. This model is underpinned by the following beliefs:

Belief #1   We are a result of our experiences, both good and bad. The brain is responsive to every experience.

Belief #2   People, not theories, are primary in relational change.

Belief #3   The brain can, and will, change for the better when trained individuals understand its basic functions and needs.

Belief #4   Relationships and ecological factors create states and traits in young people.

Belief #5   NeuroTransactional knowledge is key to transformation and resilience

Belief #6   NeuroDynamic Interventions are powerful approaches that provide positive, relational and brain-based supports to troubled young people.

This NeuroTransactional model initially seeks transformation for our troubled young people. Young people formulate beliefs and behaviors based on their prior experiences. From their perspective, they might believe, from their previous interactions, that people called "teacher", or "youth worker", or "foster parent" have always meant a "negative experience". Therefore, if your role is one of these, the assumption is that any interaction that they have with you must automatically be negative. While their view of you may seem odd, particularly if you see yourself as a caring individual, "the way that we make meaning very much influences, and perhaps even determines, how we respond" (Garfat, 2002) to different people and situations. Everybody "makes meaning" based on their previous experiences because all learning is based on prior bits of learning. This model's goal is to stretch or push challenging youth beyond the boundaries within which they normally think and feel. This change, or transformation, provides a new mindset allowing our young people to take different actions than they may have taken in the past, leading to empowerment, growth, and strength.

How We Flourish...Being Safe, Significant, Respected and Related

Our brains are naturally wired to seek out connections and relationships with others and everything that we do has a function to help support these attempts. Human beings, young and old alike, are, simply put, either looking for something that they need or want or are looking to rid themselves of something that they don't need or want. So, we enact certain behaviors and those behaviors serve as a function of meeting those needs. Because we are social beings, our brains and our selves have the ability to develop and grow in healthy ways through positive interactions with others or in negative ways through negative interactions with others. In either circumstance, we develop in direct relationship to our environmental experiences.

We believe that there are four essential elements that all humans actively seek to successfully navigate in order to flourish in their lives. They need to perceive that they are safe, significant, respected, and related to and or with others in their environments, and all our behaviour is simply our best attempt to have those needs met. We further believe that, while the sole focus of this book is not entirely the behaviour of young people, these needs are universally applicable and just as important for the adults that work with young people as for the young people themselves.

Safe

The need to perceive a sense of safety is a primary human drive. In fact, when we are alerted to any potential threat, our brains shift into what we call "survival mode". While in this mode, our brains can only focus on components associated with keeping us away from danger and allow us to approach the things that may be good for us. Danger is sent to us through our sensory systems where we perceive sight, sound, smell, taste or touch that exist within our environment. In some cases, these danger-based sensory inputs may significantly interfere with our ability to access the logical thinking systems we may need to resolve conflict or challenges that are faced in our daily lives.

Without a true perception of safety, humans are much more likely to operate within their primitive response systems. Experiencing positive connections with others allows us to increase the perception of feeling safe: safe to explore, learn, interact with others and even make mistakes without feeling threatened or scared. When we feel safe and secure with others and our environment our brains do not have to focus on being on the lookout for danger or meeting our basic needs like acquiring food, water, or shelter. Safety, especially "felt safety" involves emotional, physical, psychological and environmental elements (Moore et al., 2016). It is important to keep all of them in mind as they rarely stand in isolation! Feeling safe allows us to focus on building connections with others that can be meaningful and constructive within the framework of our lives. Safety in a school, a treatment program, or within the workplace allows us to combine our talents and abilities to experience success.

Significant

Valuable connections with others help us to emerge into who we are and feel like we are part of something bigger than ourselves. Feeling significant matters – to the point where a new field in psychology is developing solely focused upon mattering. A leader in this field, Isaac Prilleltensky (2018), explains that mattering is two-fold: people not only need to feel valued by others, they also need to feel that they add value to the world. When human beings feel like they truly matter, aggressive behaviours are reduced and pro-social behaviours increase (Pavey, Greitemeyer, & Sparks, 2011). Feeling significant in our daily lives helps us to attain the best of ourselves as we interact with the world around us.

Feeling significant has connections to an individuals' perception of personal esteem and self-worth. Stanley Coppersmith (1967) conducted an intensive study over a six-year period examining 1,748 children and their families. The highest self-esteem was found in children who felt loved and accepted, competent, in control of themselves and what happened to them, and a feeling of goodness. His findings are still relevant today (Orth, 2018).

Respected

Respect is fundamentally tied to our existence in social groups (Nader, Malloy, & Fischer, 2008). Culture shapes our brains, our identity, and influences our behaviors (Kitayama & Park, 2010). It creates a set of beliefs that we carry that include all the ideas we have about things from art and music to religion and society in general. Our beliefs about our culture can bring us together or pull us apart. Culture varies because of the different experiences that we have in our lives and there are times that we have difficulty understanding the culture of others but if we remain open-minded, we can value, embrace, and respect other perspectives. Acceptance and respect lets us believe we matter, and function effectively within the group. When those around us make no effort to understand us, ignore us, threaten us, or belittle us, we no longer feel respect and will do everything we can to severe these connections.

Related

We are born to connect and continue to seek our relationships with others from the first breath of life to the last (Cozolino 2008, Siegel 2010). We need each other. Interdependence is central to human functioning (DeKoven Fishbane, 2012), so much so that social rejection triggers physical pain in the brain (Eisenberger & Lieberman, 2004). Being alone makes us vulnerable both physically and emotionally. The Urban Dictionary contains a new word - alonement - which is defined as "that feeling that you get when you start to believe you were just meant to be alone" because life experiences have shown you that this is the only way you can live. Neurobiological, humans were never intended to be alone. We are social beings.

Being connected is a basic psychological need and once we are connected with those who allow us to feel safe, significant, and respected, we can begin to share common experiences, open ourselves to other perspectives and work together toward common goals. We can "relate" to them and them to us. Once we can relate to others, "we can walk a mile in their shoes" and learn to be compassionate and empathetic.

These four essential elements are not just necessary for the young people we work with. Adults who work with young people need to feel safe, significant, respected and related to as well. If our basic needs as adults are fulfilled we feel empowered and will have empathy for ourselves and others, a necessary skill for appropriate emotional and social intelligence as adults (Seigel, 2007, DeKoven Fishbane, 2012)

People Change People

The key thing to keep in mind as you read this book is that people are the key to transformation. Theories give us information but they do little to create lasting change. By learning more about the brain and how its systems work, you will better understand that our brain's neural pathways can change throughout life based on the connections made and the experiences had through those connections. You will be able to choose better strategies to help young people feel hope as they work towards success. We all need hope if we want to be motivated to work towards change. When we are hopeful – we look for strength instead of weakness, we work hard and keep trying – we do whatever it takes to make change happen. Hope is a two-way street. If your young people begin to experience success, a positive shift will begin and you will move from confrontation to connection. Your day to day interactions will become more positive and your connection will strengthen. Doesn't that sound motivating?

Introducing NeuroDynamic Interventions

This model supports the use of what we will call NeuroDynamic Interventions (NDIs). NDIs are a set of brain-based support strategies used by the therapeutic helper that meets the unmet developmental brain, body and experiential needs of a young person. We propose that NeuroDynamic Interventions hold the key to unlocking the requisite knowledge and skills that therapeutic helpers need to assess and work with the youth's behavioral state. They are individually based, relational and experiential opportunities that set the stage for transformation. Many of the most challenging interactions that we have with young people occur when there are problems, conflicts, stressful incidents, and inappropriate behavior. Our successful support of young people during these times will frequently come when we are able to either manage or co-manage these challenging behaviors in the moment, particularly when there is the potential of escalation into conflict or crisis. In order to do this successfully, we need to be able to understand how emotions and the brain impact behavior. NDIs use all available momentary information, helping us to take steps towards positively re-training the brain and re-shaping the experiences of our young people so that they may be more independent and successful. This momentary management provides temporary therapeutic guidance until other more long-term supports can be put in place. NeuroDynamic knowledge guides therapeutic helpers in determining whether the survival (reactive, non-thinking) or the thinking (rational, non-reactive) brain is involved and then assists them in effectively intervening in the moment, to stabilize and transform experiences.

How we approach a young person who is exhibiting challenging, oppositional, or crisis behavior is critical. Good intentions alone are not enough. NDIs provide the necessary information and skills to create opportunities for new positive experiences that in turn provide opportunities for healthy repair. For therapeutic helpers, it is critical that they fully understand and learn to manage their own responses to the thoughts, feelings, and behaviors of challenging young people. We must keep in mind, that just like youth, when adults are stressed, feeling threatened, or even just overwhelmed, their survival brains can be activated, resulting in unhealthy experiences and interactions. Therapeutic helpers bring with them their own experiences and will benefit from learning to manage them well.

We will introduce you to the fact that the survival brain is a non-thinking and purely reactive set of systems that can serve us well in times of duress but, if constantly switched-on, can cause significant coping problems. When therapeutic helpers lose their temper or behave irrationally, the young person is learning that such behavior is an acceptable way to deal with conflict, imprinting volatile experience into the brain for future use. Therapeutic helpers will benefit from being aware of their own emotional triggers, the things that young people do that can make us "see red", by not reacting without thinking. We will demonstrate that by giving both you and the young person a chance to connect with the logical brain and "get out of the survival state", both will benefit and avoid denting or damaging relationships. Just as in the safety demonstration, remember that the flight attendants remind all passengers to put on their own mask and help themselves first so that they can effectively help others. This applies when working with troubled young people as well.

The Reimbursements

Many challenging youths are missing critical experiences in their lives that are vital to optimal development, and these missing elements are often further impacted by broken relationships. Having few, to no, meaningful or safe connections to significant adults, they may seek out artificial attachments through street gangs, sexual promiscuity, attention-seeking approaches and substance abuse. They may also develop pseudo-relationships through, or with technology, drugs, or alcohol. Feelings of abandonment, hurt, and anger, may lead youth to lash out or withdraw from their environments. These makeshift attachments provide artificial "connections" that are often transitory and short-lived, not fulfilling the needs of the brain's social instincts. However, when we meet these needs appropriately, either through repairing, re-shaping, or replacing the broken or missing elements in the life of a young person, we are providing "reimbursement". This NeuroTransactional Model identifies six general areas that we have found are most often in need of reimbursement: (1) **relational**; experiences with people that have been damaging, inconsistent or absent, (2) **experiential**; missing life experiences that are typical of those in the same developmental age range critical to normal skill acquisition, (3) **biological**; basic body and health needs (4) **regulatory**; self-control and the appropriate expression of emotions and behaviour across a variety of ecologies, (5) **academic**; filling essential educational gaps that are critical for success in life, or (6) **eco-cultural**; unique experiences, beliefs, values, and language that affect interactions with others brought in from our past experiences. Young people need genuine, therapeutic helpers in their lives that are willing to provide the reimbursements through NeuroTransactional support that will start the transformation process. People can and will change if appropriate people are involved in their lives.

Person Centered Support

Carl Rogers, a well-known pioneer of person-centered therapies, believed in the potential of people and their ability to utilize opportunities that are provided to them to transform their lives. He felt that when people experience success and problem solving for themselves, they are naturally motivated to transform negative experiences into positive ones. Our NeuroTransactional model follows a similar belief system. We support the notion that when given informed, caring, and genuine adults, a challenging youth will be guided to a better life naturally through the experiences and various opportunities for reimbursement that will be available. Our model emphasizes that disconnected youth will require therapeutic helpers to guide and be with them more than most. It will be in those moments of "being with" the youth that lives will be transformed for the better. It will be in moments of "feeling with" them that we make our closest emotional connections, and in moments of "going with" them that we reshape their lives and help to shape autonomy and self-efficacy. Those who are working with disconnected youth are encouraged to utilize the natural course of opportunities throughout human development as a chance to enhance the youth's overall personal strength and well-being, as well as those that are structured through the reimbursement process.

Relational Optimism

Elizabeth Phelps and her colleagues at New York University studied the impact of optimistic thinking on the brain (Sharot, et al., 2007). The study indicated that simply asking people to think of positive events in the future significantly increased activity in the anterior cingulate cortex (ACC), an area of the brain that usually regulates the impact of emotion on memory and decision making. In contrast to these findings, prior studies showed that depressed, negative people usually have lower ACC activity levels.

It is further believed that positive, meaningful relationships can reactivate processing and pathways in the brain and actually change its structure for the better. The purpose of the NeuroTransactional model is to provide hope to both therapeutic helpers and challenging youth. Through this optimistic approach, we can establish a "hopeful" culture-led and enhanced by therapeutic planning. Hopeful cultures positively support challenging youth and foster positive change. We believe that everyone has the potential to be that agent of hopeful change!

Dopamine - The Hopeful Neurotransmitter

Current research in neuroscience is suggesting that through positive connections and interactions with others, dopamine, a neurotransmitter in our brains, may play an important role in the building of pathways to change. Historically, dopamine has long been associated with general pleasure and reward. Scientists believed that dopamine was produced only when a reward was actively sought (Berridge & Robinson, 1998) and that the brain responded to the reward stimulus by producing certain levels of dopamine. Current research enhances this by adding that dopamine predicts the desirability, or lack of, an outcome which in turn motivates us towards, or away, from that outcome (Bromberg-Martin, Matsumoto, & Hikosaka, 2010). It is not only associated with, but plays a large role in human motivation. In essence, this is a chemical that regulates a variety of functions within the brain and the body and is essential to not only surviving but to surviving well.

Scientists have known for many years that dopamine has a greater impact on learning behavior than originally thought, but they were not sure why. Recent findings suggest that dopamine directly impacts learning and change through chemically-based motivation. Researchers have discovered that dopamine encourages people to attempt to achieve an outcome and persevere even in the face of a little adversity before they actually have ever achieved that goal because they simply believe there is the possibility of success (Daw & Shohamy, 2008). It is not the achievement itself that produces the majority of the dopamine but rather the possibility of achieving the outcome (Bromberg- Martin, Matsumoto, & Hikosaka, 2010). Dopamine is being released in larger quantities before the goal is achieved - creating a chemical motivation to move forward towards change.

If dopamine has the power to create the motivation for us to try something new, it also provides us with a new sense of hope. Once we have the hope of success and the motivation to achieve it - we are more easily able to embrace change and move towards transformation. In the PersonBrain Model, we see this process as a sequential journey:

Hope -> Motivation -> Transformation -> Resilience

Today's professionals are faced with ever-increasing demands to meet a greater diversity of needs and challenging behaviors of young people. These challenging behaviors often occur when the young people we work with do not have the skills to meet their needs and/or the ability to communicate to us that they need help meeting those needs. Their prior experiences have left them feeling hopeless. A multitude of scientific disciplines are now proving that when provided with appropriate knowledge and targeted strategies, adults create experiences that allow these young people to feel hope and motivation to work towards more positive outcomes. The adults become extremely powerful agents of transformation, even in the most serious of cases.

From Transformation to Resilience

Empowerment, growth, and strength lead to the ultimate goal – resilience. Resilience is the ability to withstand the "bumps in the road" that life hands us, to adapt well in the face of adversity, stress, and trauma. It is not something that we are born with. It is through our behaviors, thoughts, and actions that we can learn and develop skills from positive experiences in supportive relationships. The supportive focus becomes centered upon recreating new experiences or making new meaning. In the future, when the same young person hears those words, other more positive memories arise due to new experiences that have been provided for them by a therapeutic helper

People implementing the NeuroTransactional model become "therapeutic helpers" for those with whom they engage in relationships and experiences. Therapeutic helpers are the people who help create experiences that are transformative, positive and brain changing. But, they must have the knowledge of how to work with others and to connect and/or interact with challenging young people who need them the most. Therapeutic helpers play significant roles because they are there with us, they feel with us, and they go with us. They are there for the long haul. No matter who you are, you can play a role in being therapeutic by "being with, feeling with, and going with" the young people you work with, live with, or with whom you interact.

The Advent of Positive Psychology

Until the middle of the 20th century, neuroscientists and psychologists had considered the brain and nervous system to operate only as independent biological systems. They ignored the significant impact that the social environment has on human interactions. But for some, the focus started to shift. Most psychologists had operated in the disease or deficit model. However, some believed in a more positive model that focused on optimal functioning. The move away from the "deficit perspective" of psychology to what is now known as "positive psychology" had slowly begun. The deficit perspective saw problems within the child, with little or no time spent looking at the child's environment. It focused on what has "gone wrong". In contrast, positive psychology focuses on what has "gone right" for the child and in his ecology when assessing, diagnosing, and intervening with youth who are experiencing difficulties.

Abraham Maslow - Meeting Basic Needs

In the 1940s, Abraham Maslow, a pioneer of humanistic psychology (a holistic approach to human existence) focused on what motivated, directed, and sustained human behavior. He developed what has become known as a hierarchy of needs: physiological, safety, love and belonging, esteem, and self-actualization. Maslow believed that the most basic level of needs must be met before an individual would be motivated to aspire to the higher-level needs. Maslow also coined the term "meta motivation" to describe the motivation of people who go beyond their basic needs and strive for something better (Maslow, 1954). Maslow found that emotionally healthy individuals tend to have "peak experiences" in life, times when a person might report being at his or her happiest, which lead to some sort of transformation (Jacobs, 2003).

Urie Bronfenbrenner -The Importance of Ecology

In the 1960s, psychologist Urie Bronfenbrenner developed an ecological systems theory to explain that a child's growth and development are affected by everything in a child and in the child's environment. He considered all the different aspects of the environment (the child's ecology) that influence his development, including the immediate relationships or organizations with which the child interacts (microsystem); how the different parts of a child's microsystem work together for the sake of the child (mesosystem);

and the other people and the other influential people and places with which a child interacts indirectly such as parents' workplaces, extended family members, or the community (exosystem). The more encouraging and nurturing these relationships and places were the better the child's growth and overall well-being. In addition, Brofenbrenner also took into consideration the macrosystem, which was the largest and least direct part of the child's ecology but which still had a great influence over a child. The macrosystem included things such as the government, cultural values, and the economy (Bronfenbrenner, 1979). His ecological systems model changed the way many social and behavioral scientists approached the study of people and their environments.

The Social Brain . . . A New Frontier

In the early 1990s, psychologists John Cacioppo and Gary Berntson encouraged a research partnership between psychologists and neuroscientists. From this collaboration came an interdisciplinary field, social neuroscience, devoted to understanding how biological systems implement social processes and behavior, and to using biological concepts and methods to inform and refine theories of social processes and behavior.

In a similar vein, Daniel Siegel, a psychiatrist and professor at the UCLA School of Medicine, combined discoveries from the fields of cognitive neuroscience and psychology, creating an "integrated view of how human development occurs within the social world in transaction with the functions of the brain that gives rise to the mind" — interpersonal neurobiology (2001, p.67). Interpersonal neurobiology studies what occurs in the brain as a result of significant life experiences and how relationships and experiences can be used to actually change the brain in positive ways.

Daniel Goleman, author of *Social Intelligence*, notes that our brains are the only biological system in our bodies that continually attune to, and become influenced by, the internal states of those around us. In fact, "our social interactions play a role in reshaping our brain through 'neuroplasticity,' which means that repeated experiences sculpt the shape, size, and number of neurons and their synaptic connections" (2006, p.11).

Attunement –"Feeling Felt"

From our first breath of life, connections to others become important. When we are properly able to connect with others, momentarily or over an extended period, we learn various aspects of their individual nuances. We attune to some or all of them. Attunement involves recognizing aspects that are either good or bad. Attunement means being "in sync" with others so that we can better connect and survive. When we engage in these kinds of attuned relationships with others, our brains develop regulatory circuits that allow us to exert self-control and engage empathetically with others (Siegel, 2007).

Through attunement, we can, over time, begin to empathetically understand others' feelings and needs. Empathy is the integration of information gleaned by observing body language, reading emotional signals and then making sense of others' feelings through our thoughts and beliefs. From empathy we can move to the next step - compassion. While empathy is a more passive response, an understanding of feelings without necessarily any action on our part, compassion requires that we take positive action to alleviate a person's pain or situation. It also means that we can help another without becoming overwhelmed ourselves.

Many young people suffer from a "not good enough" level of attunement that causes them to misread or misinterpret the intentions of others. This may mean that they perceive the world as either an overtly safe or a threatening place to be. They lack the necessary NeuroTransactional balance to navigate the world safely and need positive relationships with therapeutic helpers that allow them to experience the attunement and experience, empathy and compassion being demonstrated first-hand.

The findings of "hopeful" psychologists have helped us to understand that our past experiences do not need to dictate who we will be forever. Through other experiences and relationships, we continue to re-shape and repair our brains. Our brains are always capable of change. The brain is particularly changeable through experiences and relationships, and new and positive experiences and relationships can create new pathways that override the past.

Attunement and attachment are words that are often used interchangeably and they are not the same. We attune ourselves through an initial brain/body connection that we feel with another person. We will then spend a great deal of time with people figuring each other out, sharing experiences and a range of emotions that help enhance a relationship, which we call bonding. Think of bonding as "emotional glue" or "feeling felt" by others. It is the set of experiences that take place around and between people that will lead to a more permanent emotional connection or attachment. We learn to bond and attach as infants and the lessons we learn through those experiences becomes the template for how we attach with others throughout our life.

What Makes an Interaction Therapeutic?

Just because something is called therapeutic doesn't mean that it is. With therapy, there is no "one size fits all" experience or relationship when working with people and their brains. Due to experiences past and present, each youth will have separate and unique needs that must be met by therapeutic helpers. In many cases, caregivers with positive intentions will seek out "therapy" for their troubled youth at any cost. A person called psychologist, counselor, or social worker often does this. The immediate intention of the caregiver is that arranging sessions with people holding a recognizable mental health degree will automatically result in transformation. In actuality, research is proving that it is a relationship with a caring and trusted person that is most critical in therapeutically transforming youth, not so much the specific methods that are used (Bernard, 2004). The NeuroTransactional transactions between people and their ecologies are critical in transformation. The importance of these transactions is frequently overlooked - often because they seem so minor and unsubstantial in the moment. However, it is these types of micro-interactions that are most responsible for constructing the macro-relationship between the therapeutic helper and the youth that leads to change.

It has been said that the definition of insanity is doing the same thing over and over again, and expecting different results. The same would hold true of sending a youth from psychologist to psychologist or counselor to counselor with nothing positive resulting from the interactions, but expecting the young person to change. When dealing with disconnected young people we often think that a referral for therapy may be helpful. However, just referring someone to therapy does not ensure success. Most disconnected youths have been to see multiple therapists and many of them have been placed in some form of mental health institution. In many cases, these experiences have proven to be of little therapeutic help to them. For many youth, the numerous experiences of not being helped have become entrenched in the brain. These negative experiences of not being helped will remain until new people and experiences reimburse them with something to the contrary. People change people, and experiences with people change the brain.

Therapy is a type of interactive experience, and experiences change the brain. For transactions to be positive, the brain must interpret the experience as "good." When the brain recognizes the goodness in the experience, the brain changes for the better, but in bad interactions, the brain can be changed for the worse. Consider the following situation: Damien, an alternative high school student, was sitting at his desk at the beginning of the first period, head down while the rest of the group was working. His teacher walked over to his desk and quietly asked if he needed some help getting started. Unbeknownst to her, Damien had just experienced a big fight with his new stepdad, whom he has never really gotten along with, before coming to school, and he was upset and very angry. He lost control, leaped up, grabbed his binder, threw it, and cursed the teacher using very sexually explicit language. This was not the first time that Damien had lost control at school. In fact, his history in that program had been tumultuous at best. He had had a difficult history in traditional schools and his experience with teachers and administrators had been extremely negative. He was convinced that all school staff hated him and did everything in their power to get rid of him as soon as they could. While Damien's loss of control was not new to the alternative staff, he had never shown this level of disrespect before. The class was shocked and silent - waiting for the teacher's response.

One of two things would happen - both with very different impacts on Damien's brain and his way of viewing the world around him. The teacher could have become counter-aggressive, yelling at Damien for his offensive language, and had him suspended. This would have reinforced in Damien's mind and the pathways in his brain, that he was right - all teachers hated him and wanted him gone. Instead, the teacher stood silently and waited until Damien stopped yelling and swearing. Realizing that there was likely more to the situation than she was aware of, calmly and quietly she asked if there was anything she could do. He responded that he just wanted to get out of there. She told him that was fine and to come back when he was ready. The teacher then called home, explained what had happened to a parent and reinforced the idea that he was welcome to return when he was ready. It took him several days before he returned to the building. Upon arrival, he checked in with an administrator who told him he must deal with the teacher directly. Damien was reluctant from his past experiences, but he did go to see the teacher. He opened the conversation with, "Guess I'm kicked out, huh?" The teacher asked him if he wanted to be "kicked out" which Damien found quite puzzling. After a moment of thought, he said he didn't. Finding a quiet place to chat, the teacher sat down with Damien and talked about what had happened. Damien opened up a little about the fight with his stepdad and they used a few minutes to talk about more productive ways of dealing with stress and anger. When it was time to return to class, Damien commented that he was very surprised that he had been allowed back and would try to make sure he didn't "blow" his chance. The next time Damien was stressed in class, the outcome was better. Damien's positive experience allowed his brain to create new pathways. Not only did he begin to work on more productive coping strategies, but he began to see that not all teachers were out to get him.

Therapeutic helpers must constantly assess the effectiveness of the strategies, interactions, and reimbursements that are being used. Constantly looking for new ways to reach and connect is essential in proving to youth that you are different and that by working together things can be better than they were previously.

The Eco-Relational Funnel

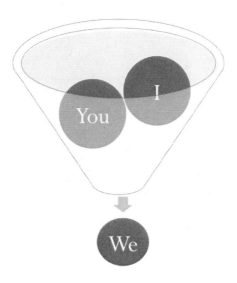

Graphically speaking, the Eco-Relational funnel is a way of explaining what happens to the "neural pathways of experience" between two people when they come together within an environment. The funnel represents the particular ecologies in which a youth exists.

The ecologies would have many layers, much like those that Urie Bronfenbrenner described: their immediate relationships or organizations; how the different parts of a child's immediate ecology work together for the sake of the child; the other people and places that the child may not interact with directly but that still have a large effect on him; and other organizations or ideologies that impact his life.

The "I" Experience

The "I" experience is what the child or youth brings into the interaction by way of their brain and body. This is primarily his or her past experience, what he or she brings to the table based on life experiences up to now. The people, events, and environments that have shaped the brain will now be colliding with those experiences of the therapeutic helper, although it will include present experiences.

The "You" Experience

The "you" experience is what you, the therapeutic helper, bring into the relational transaction by way of your brain and body. This involves all your past experiences and the present in which you find yourself, as well as your expected experiences in the future.

The "We" Experience

The "we" experience is what happens when the "you" and "I" collide, forming two merged experiences that evolve into a shared experience. We cannot help but to have our experiences collide; it is only natural. Thom Garfat (2008), a noted expert in child and youth care, calls the work that is done between the "I" and "You" the relational "in-between." This is important to remember, as *every time* a therapeutic helper interacts with a youth, a new opportunity for healing and transformation becomes possible. Like all other experiences and relationships, this can be good or bad. Therapeutic helpers have a significant role in implementing positive experiences for youth who challenge us in the present because of their prior disconnections.

Diversity and Belonging

Young people come to us with unique sets of experiences, strengths, and ideas based upon how they have lived their lives. These differences can be along the lines of race, religion, political beliefs, socio-economic status, ethnicity, ability, gender, or sexual orientation. As therapeutic helpers, it will be important to explore and incorporate a variety of perspectives in how we interact with our young people and be able to offer them different ways of looking and interacting within their various environments.

Earlier in this chapter, we discussed the four essential elements that are needed for people to flourish: safety, significance, respect and being related.

Stop for a moment and think back. All of us can remember a moment when we felt like we didn't fit in or didn't belong. We remember it because it hurt - being excluded was painful then and even thinking about it now dredges up that pain again. Were you the last one picked for a team? Were you the one who had an accent when you moved to a new country? Did you have to hide religious beliefs or your sexual orientation from neighbours or colleagues? Hiding your authentic self just to fit in is exhausting and does not make you feel safe, significant, respected or related (Kawamoto et al., 2015). Your focus is on survival and not on growth or development.

While there is no standard solution, social sensitivity and working collaboratively is needed if everyone is to feel psychologically safe enough to be themselves and encourage others to do the same. History has repeatedly shown us, often through acts of extreme violence, what happens when people feel excluded. In order to flourish; to feel safe, significant, respected, and related, we all need to create an environment where both young people and the adults who work with them have the following (Baumeister & Leary, 1995, Stillman & Baumeister, 2009).

1. A sense of relatedness - knowing that you are safe being yourself
2. A purpose - you have an active role, a significant part of the group
3. A voice - the ability to voice your opinions and be respected even if your ideas are different
4. A sense of inclusion - you are part of a group working for a common goal - what you do is directly related to those in your group

The acceptance and promotion of diversity, maximized inclusion and authentic relatedness allows everyone to realize their potential in a rewarding and motivating manner by creating safe spaces to grow and learn. Without this sense of overall safety, people are constrained and are not able to reach their fullest potential.

Relational Ecology

The relational ecology consists of all those people in our past, present, and expected future. Under normal developmental circumstances, most people believe that they will have reasonably secure relationships in their future. However, young people who have had poor relational experiences in the past or present tend to see their future as unfulfilled and not worth working for. The NeuroTransactional approach attempts to correct this thinking and demonstrate strength and capability within these young people that offer offers hope by simply being a part of their experience.

Being a part of their experience is a good start but it is not the only key to effectively working with troubled young people. It is extremely important for therapeutic helpers to assess their personal states *prior* to engaging with youth. This must be done consciously. We assume that we do this but most of us do not. It must be done in order to prepare the adult brain for the potential challenges ahead. If you have buttons that are easily pushed, prepare for them to be pushed and develop a plan on how you will respond professionally. Failure to prepare will leave you vulnerable and the youth without the needed support he/she deserves. Remember, this is why you are there in the first place. Failure to adequately prepare oneself as a therapeutic helper prior to interacting with a youth in a difficult interaction may result in a damaged experience, reinforcing a youth's belief system that adults are not effective helpers. It is critical that therapeutic helpers have this personal awareness and self-control in order to effectively provide corrective experiences that reshape neural pathways in a positive manner.

Scaffold for Support

Much as scaffolding serves as a secure foundation in the construction process, therapeutic helpers can also provide a similar kind of emotional support. Many of our challenging young people want to talk about their problems and concerns but may find it difficult or impossible if their prior experiences have convinced them that adults are not trustworthy or safe. When youth find therapeutic helpers who they feel genuinely care for them and trust begins to develop, they will start to share their personal narratives (stories). Their narratives open a window into their lives and experiences and give us insight into how their brains and private knowledge about the world have developed. Public knowledge is what youth want us to know at that particular moment. In many cases, the young person will protect their private knowledge, releasing bits and pieces of it to us slowly. They need to know their stories are safe with us and that we can be trusted to help them with the information they share. We believe that the youth should serve as his or her best life story expert, both personally and to others. After all, we have not lived their life so allowing them to tell their story at a safe and comfortable pace will ultimately yield a stronger relationship and a deeper understanding of the youth's life story.

Together we build a structure of therapeutic support or emotional scaffolding that creates an opportunity for young people to safely disclose and share the information that they believe is important safely. On some occasions, young people with limited positive connections may initially find the therapeutic helper to be something new, exciting, and safe. This sense of newness and safety may prompt them to impulsively want to build the relational scaffold "50 stories high" by quickly telling you everything they can possibly remember in one sitting. For those that will try to build too fast, we will have to encourage them to slow down and remind them that we hope to have time to build this event together. Reminding them that there is plenty of time for sharing reinforces your commitment to them in the future. This helps to prevent too much information from coming too quickly, which may cause us to overlook important details of the life story. It will be these details in their life that will provide clues and inform how we will design the reimbursements.

The Therapeutic Dialogue

Encouraging the disclosure of information is best taken in a natural way, over time as your relationship strengthens and trust is formed. Building the "scaffold" together is key in the supportive experience. According to Baker (2007), "People tell their stories in therapeutic interactions. This is how they explain themselves. But they *also* learn to tell stories — to organize and make something whole from often-chaotic feelings of pain and confusion. The enterprise of therapy is itself a kind of story" (p.706).

Glauser and Bozarth (2001) describe the ability to empathically listen as an "extratherapeutic" variable, emphasizing the therapeutic helper's ability to understand the youth's world while validating their personhood and facilitating the relationship in a way that promotes growth and development. Providing this extratherapeutic support helps to prevent therapeutic helpers from engaging in what Smith and Steindler (1993, p.110) called therapeutic zeal — "a kind of misguided conviction that they must provide treatment literally at all costs."

Trust Trials

A wise person once said, "it takes years to build trust and seconds to destroy it." If you have ever had anyone betray your trust, particularly family or a very close friend that feels like family, you truly understand that quote. Trust is the foundation for connecting positively with youth. Trust has a positive impact on relationships; lack of trust has a negative impact. Without trust, relationships remain stagnant and unable to jump over the hurdles that are necessary for personal growth.

Trust trials are opportunities youth provide to us and we provide to them to prove we are worthy of the other's trust. These trials are frequently quite intense and test our resolve to stay committed to the youths who challenge us. When we prove that we are committed to being with them for the long haul, they begin to see us as being more permanent strengths in their lives. According to Carl Rogers (1951) trust and true concern can only be communicated if the youth or therapeutic helper perceives it to be genuine and "feels" that there exists a trusting connection.

Trust trials come in many forms from youth, testing our therapeutic resolve to continue to be with, feel with, and go with youth throughout their time with us. Screaming, cursing, resisting, and even physical aggression can be a part of the trust trial. As a therapeutic helper, we always remember that the youth brings unique past experiences into the current relational mix. When dealing with very challenging youth, we must be ready for any behavior that the youth feels is necessary to test our genuineness and ability to help. These youth will use their experiences when putting us through trust trials. It is all they have. In turn, we will use our experiences to react or interact with them in some way. It is here that the way we respond will determine whether trust forms or fails to take shape at all. Will you be like the others that have failed them in the past? Or will you be someone who reshapes experience and helps to make things better?

Trust will be earned over time and may not come easily. It is the therapeutic helper's responsibility to convince the youth that he or she is worth the time and effort, even if experiences, cultural differences, and virtues collide uncomfortably. The behavior exhibited by the therapeutic helper, non-verbal and verbal, will play a significant role in conveying genuine care and concern as the brain is reading the small cues that are being broadcast by the therapeutic helper. There is no winner in the trust trial process, only the building of new experiences that are shaped by the interactions between the youth and therapeutic helper.

The Experiential Mosaic

A mosaic is an art form that typically consists of broken bits and pieces of glass, tile, or other objects that are relatively meaningless alone but when assembled in just the right way, can take on a meaningful form. The same holds true for disconnected youth. When the right person comes along and helps them to assemble the various bits and pieces of their life, a special and amazing "mosaic" emerges. Much like the artistic mosaic, young people will need therapeutic helpers in their lives to help put the bits and pieces of their experiential mosaic together.

The experiential mosaic attempts to serve as a visual analogy of those "key" individuals and experiences that have played, are playing or will play a significant role in the youth's past, present, and expected future. Like pieces of glass or stone that form the mosaic, people and experiences become critical in forming a "true" picture of who has been in, who is in, and who may be in the life of the youth. Once the therapeutic helper and the youth have had enough experience together, the mosaic becomes more complete and understandable.

Each piece of glass within the mosaic seems insignificant when it stands alone, but once the various pieces come together, the picture is clearer. We must pay careful attention to the experiences and people in the youth's life that ultimately make up the mosaic.

Within a NeuroTransactional model, we must be aware of how the full range of relational experiences can prove to be diagnostic in relation to how the brain has organized itself. The impact that these relationships have had on brain development is critical in understanding why youth behave the way they do under varying circumstances. If our brains are social organs that develop and grow through experiences, then our initial experiences and relationships are critical to what happens later in life. Attachment theory provides a model for analyzing the impact of relationships and experiences on the developing brain and personality. The findings of social neuroscience and interpersonal neurobiology suggest that we are hard-wired to connect (Siegel, 2001). We have an inborn attachment system that enhances our ability to survive by recruiting the assistance and resources of our primary caregivers.

Newborn babies are anything but passive beings. They come with reflexive actions equipped to connect with their primary caregivers (Cozolino, 2006). As a child grows, there are four unique characteristics of attachment: (a) proximity maintenance - the desire to be near the people we are attached to, (b) safe haven - returning to the attachment figure for comfort and safety in the face of a fear or threat, (c) secure base - the attachment figure acts as a base of security from which the child can explore the surrounding environment, and (d) separation distress - anxiety that occurs in the absence of the attachment figure. These create early relational patterns that become internalized and shape our brains and who we become. In other words, early relationships and experiences become wired in the brain and later function as unconscious templates that affect and guide us through life.

Life Experiences and Poverty

Growing and developing in optimal environments with diverse opportunities allows an individual to achieve their best physical and mental health, and social and economic potential. We have long understood the relationship between growing up in poverty and less than optimal brain development (Lipina & Colombo, 2009), diminished health over the life span (Gilbert et el al., 2010) and economic disadvantage (Fang et al, 2012), but less research has been focused on the experiences of poverty and the impact of the learning environment on children's attitude towards school and their perceived value of education.

Multiple studies done by the Joseph Rowntree Foundation's education and poverty researchers found that children's' experiences in school differ for less advantaged children as compared to their more affluent peers in the following ways:

- Children growing up in poverty felt less control over their education and that while they saw an advantage in having an education, their disaffected attitudes towards school and teachers hindered their progress (Horgan, 2007, Sutton et al., 2007).
- Many disaffected young people developed strong perceptions about mistreatment leading to generalized resentments about school from their historical experiences in other environments (Frankham et al., 2007).
- Homework was problematic for children growing up in poverty as they often had to deal with noisy and chaotic environments and parents that were unable to assist when they encountered problems (Kellett & Dar, 2007).
- Extra-curricular activities that provide auxiliary learning experiences were not as readily available for less advantaged young people (Wikeley et al., 2007).

Thomson and Russell, 2007 found that relationships were the key feature needed to re-engage disaffected children with education. They found that, to be successful, those working with disaffected children needed to build relationships not only with the child, but with the families, if possible, and other educators. They believe that building these new relationships that address feelings of powerlessness and disengagement will allow disadvantaged children to feel more in control of their education.

Attachment and the Brain

Attachment theorists John Bowlby (1969/1982) and Mary Ainsworth (1978) believed that every child needs a healthy attachment to caregivers who are empathetic and responsive to the child's needs. When caretakers provide environments or ecologies where there is consistent sensitivity and attunement to the needs of their children, they are providing what Bowlby called a secure base. Children can count on those caregivers for comfort and attention when they are upset. This idea was taken a step further by Ainsworth when she proposed that they also need a safe haven or an emotionally secure place, that they can return to after any new life experience. Unfortunately, the lack of well-attuned caretakers and children who do not form secure attachments means not all children are afforded these enriched experiences.

Although early childhood attachment experiences do have a large effect on growth and development, and despite earlier scientific consensus that the brain is fixed and unchangeable by adolescence, social neuroscientists now know that the brain is changeable, or "plastic." Whenever we have an experience, neurons, the cells in our brain, fire. Every time neurons fire there is the potential to strengthen and/or create new pathways or synapses. When neurons fire, it is even possible to stimulate the growth of new neurons that can impact future experiences. Neuroscientists call this neurogenesis. When new neurons and new pathways are created in conjunction with experience, it is called neuroplasticity. We now know our brains have a lifelong ability to restructure their neural pathways based on experience and any meaningful relationship can reactivate neuroplastic processes and actually change the structure of the brain (Cozolino, 2006).

Allan Schore, a leading researcher in the field of neuropsychology, believes that nurturing relationships with any significant adult can play a big role in the brain's ability to change (1994). Repeated early experiences certainly sculpt and strengthen our neural pathways, but nurturing and therapeutic relationships later in life can, to some extent, re-write and re-sculpt the pathways laid down initially. These therapeutic relationships and experiences can have a repairing effect and, in essence, can provide the secure emotional base and safe haven that is missing. As a therapeutic helper, other significant adults in a child's life can provide open, attuned, non-judgmental experiences in a safe and secure place and repair and re-route those early neural pathways.

Our Hopeful Genes

Just as our brains can change through new and positive interactions, we now also know that our genes are no longer necessarily our destiny. The study of epigenetics is the new science of how our genes are expressed. This is an area that holds great hope for the development of interventions that can aid in NeuroTransactional changes that "switch on" helpful genes. We used to believe that our genes solely dictated instructions for building and running a body. We now know that it is a two-way street. The body (nature), and the environment (nurture), can change the way that our genes are expressed (when and how much) as well as, potentially, how they are passed on. Findings from epigenetic research help us to understand individual differences resulting from life experiences. Studies done on identical twins, who have exactly the same genetic makeup but different physiological or behavioral responses or disease susceptibility, support the idea that both nature and nurture affect not only who we are but also who we can become.

Geneticists had known for years that the DNA inside each cell's nucleus needed a little extra something to tell the genes what to do. They also believed that these changes only occurred during fetal development. But the groundbreaking work of scientists in the early 1990s showed us that DNA could be altered even in our adult years. Geneticists understood that changes in diet or exposure to certain chemicals could set off a cascade of cellular (epigenetic) changes. However, they were shocked to find that epigenetic change could be passed down from parent to child, one generation to the next.

Using this information, two scientists (Moshe Szyf, a molecular biologist and geneticist at McGill University in Montreal and Michael Meany, a McGill neurobiologist) met in a bar in Spain in 1992 and asked a very important question: If diet and chemicals can cause epigenetic changes, could certain experiences — child neglect, drug abuse or other severe stresses — also set off epigenetic changes to the DNA inside the neurons of a person's brain? Their research led to a new field, behavioral epigenetics. Through the study of behavioral epigenetics, we now know that traumatic experiences in our past, or in our recent ancestors' past, leave molecular "tags" on our DNA. Our experiences and those of our relatives can reside in our genes. It is possible that we can inherit not only our relatives' physical characteristics — we can also inherit their behavioral and psychological temperaments. Or not. Remember that it is a two-way street. Despite your genetic predisposition, the environment in which you grow up and the ways in which those around you nurture you will affect whether or not those epigenetic markers are actually expressed. Epigenetic changes are a response to a stressful environment, and if that environmental stress is eliminated, then over time the DNA will return to its original state.

Research continues to uncover connections between epigenetic change and various factors in our environments. As our knowledge of epigenetics grows, we continue to learn more about how the way we live influences the way our genes are expressed. There is a lot yet to learn, but what we do know is that we are a combination of both nature and nurture.

What Is Memory?

Simply stated, memory is about how our brain and body remember bits and pieces from our past so that these bits and pieces can be reactivated to our advantage in the future. There are various forms of memory that assist us in going through life, and memory is closely affiliated with the act of learning. In learning, one ideally takes a look at specific facts of a situation and applies them in a way that is helpful. Memory works in a similar way. All learning is based upon prior learning and all memory is based, to some degree, on prior memories. Nancy Andreasen (2005), chair of psychiatry at the University of Iowa, states that each person is comprised of forty-six chromosomes and approximately thirty thousand genes that have somehow come together by the merger of a male and female parent. This merger results in the unique and individualized development of the actual person and his or her various parts (liver, heart, eye color, etc.). No one enters the world and remains exactly the same throughout life. The design of the brain must also be understood in this context. It develops from a combination of both the nature and nurture of the individual with memories resulting from multiple and complex cell connections based upon genetics and experience.

The content of those memories becomes important as the person develops and grows. Through their daily interactions with others (how they respond to a simple question or task for example), people display their experiential memories. Whether learning data or learning social cues, memory is critical in helping us to hold on to important information in the present that could be beneficial to us in the future. Without memory, we would be constantly experiencing "newness," which would prove to be detrimental to our existence. In essence, we would never learn from our successes or failures. We would just "be" in the moment.

Explicit and Implicit Memories

Explicit Memory

Memories can be explicit or implicit. Explicit memories are memories that can easily be consciously recalled and verbalized. Explicit memories can be semantic (knowledge of data or facts in isolation and not connected to any particular event) such as a list of dates or capital cities that you need to memorize for a history test or the multiplication tables many of us memorized in elementary school. Explicit memories can also be episodic (personal life events connected to other people or events) such as your first kiss, or where you were when the planes hit the World Trade Center. We use this type of memory to remember our daily schedule or what we did last summer.

Implicit Memory

Implicit memory is a type of memory in which early or previous experiences are encoded without conscious awareness. Implicit memories can be as simple as remembering how to do something without conscious awareness (like tying your shoes or riding a bike) or more complex social memories. These memories are not consciously thought about but are demonstrated in our attitudes and behaviors. A strong emotional reaction to someone you have never met before is an example of implicit memories in action (Cozolino, 2006).

We are born with immature brains and our first experiences with parents or caretakers become our earliest memories. These elements of sensations, perceptions and images are implicit memories – memories that form the basis of our mental model of our environment. Continued experiences in life allow us to create generalized non-verbal conclusions about the world around us, and these conclusions guide our on-going perceptions and actions (Badenoch, 2008). While explicit memories are contextual to a time and place, implicit memories are not. When implicit memories are activated, we believe that they are there because of something happening in the present when in fact we are interpreting a present-day experience with the mental models we created in the past. Implicit memories and the mental models they create can give us a perceptual bias, impacting behavior and how we approach certain situations. Because they are unconscious, we can be unaware that they are, in fact, driving our behavior, and possibly making us look quite irrational in the eyes of those around us.

Memories ... Opportunities for Change

Daniel Siegel (1999) reminds us that every time something is recalled it has the potential to be modified. So, remembering actually opens the door to potential transformation. This provides a tremendous "in the moment" opportunity to the therapeutic helper in the restructuring of experiences that are eventually stored within the brain. Therapeutic helpers are provided with moments to instill empathy, compassion and comfort to even the most painful of memories. We know that new memories strengthen neural pathways in the brain. The more we engage in a task the more it becomes seeded within our memory systems. If a youth is exposed to violent and threatening environments and people, the brain shapes itself to match the experience. If a youth is exposed to positive and supportive relational and ecological systems, the brain develops in a positive and adaptive manner.

Recent work in the field of neurobiology has revealed that epigenetic processes are essential for complex brain functions. In animal studies, researchers found that some of the chemicals that alter DNA are needed to allow proper functioning of signals to the brain that affect memory and learning. How well memories are formed and stored depends upon the strength of the connections between pathways (neurons) in the brain. The stronger this connection, the stronger the memory formation and retrieval (Alarcon et al., 2004).

The chemicals that help form and store the memories also affect the direct formation and retention of cellular and behavioral responses to fear and stress-related memories. While the impact that these chemicals can have is wide-ranging and diverse, it is interesting to note that some of these epigenetic mechanisms appear to help in one form of memory creation and retention that actually encourage certain harmful aspects of memory, such as the chronic replay of fearful memories (Mikaelsson & Miller, 2011, Roth & Sweatt, 2009).

NeuroTransactional Support

We have indicated that positive NeuroTransactional interactions can help change the brain for the better, both in the therapeutic helper and the youth in need. In this model, we call this process NeuroTransactional support. NeuroTransactional support occurs when a therapeutic helper recreates and transforms relationships and experiences through natural opportunities to retrain the brain into more positive, adaptive, and functional ways through purposefully planned, needs-based interactions with disconnected youth. People are the key to this transformation. The focus is on the experiences that are shared. These interactions show the youth that we genuinely want to help. They encourage a respectful interchange and relationship between the therapeutic helper and the youth. The young person is no longer the *sole* focus of the transformative process as people must now assume therapeutically specific roles in providing the youth with what it is he or she needs across a wide spectrum. Because development across a lifespan is fluid, memories are subject to continuously changing experiences. Relationship interactions change the structure of the brain and the brain adapts accordingly because it is designed to transform to meet the needs of the world around it.

Story - Krista: Creating New Files

Krista's mother was recently remarried when Krista, 13 years old, arrived at the school. The three year divorce period had been protracted and messy and Krista's mom was spending a great deal of time with her new husband. Krista had spent many years feeling that neither parent really loved her and that she was part of the reason they divorced. Her new step-father struggled to connect with Krista as she blamed him for the break-up. Both her mom and step-dad had tried to compensate with material things and money, but not by spending much time with her. By the time we met Krista she was feeling unloved and ignored and was using the money her parents gave her to self-medicate with a variety of drugs. She was bitter, angry, and resentful.

Whenever Krista did not get what she wanted, she would launch into a tirade of abuse or simply not show up to school for days on end. Her teacher tried many different ways to connect with Krista with varying degrees of success. Although her attendance wasn't stellar, every time Krista reappeared at school, the teacher would welcome her back and ask her about her time away. Attempts were consistently made to include her in the activities of the school despite her on-going refusal to "do that sucky crap". For almost two years, she gave the entire staff a run for their money, swearing at them, skipping classes, and getting other students involved in her "declarations of independence". One day, in a particularly abusive mood, she looked at her teacher who was calmly trying to settle her down and burst into tears. While crying she yelled, "I have done everything to make you hate me. Why won't you just leave me alone? Go away!" The teacher smiled and told her that she was a member of this school, one of our students and that we didn't go away, but we could respect her need for physical space. We were in this together. They sat and talked while Krista collected herself. Following that afternoon, the teacher saw small changes. Krista's attendance improved a little, her outbursts were less frequent and less abusive, and her attitude improved a little. The teacher was hopeful that a corner had been turned – and then the bottom fell out. Krista ended up in the hospital, barely surviving a drug overdose. When she returned to school, she sat with her teacher and told her that even though she had screwed up again, she knew that at least she could come back to school because the teachers there were really stubborn and never gave up. Krista had a way to go but the first steps had been taken. She started attending classes on a regular basis and started attending a girl's group at the school to deal with her issues with her parents.

As the days progressed, interactions between Krista and the teacher began to create new "files" in her memory system, now allowing her greater opportunity to recall positive experiences with adults and increase the likelihood of greater trust and connection. Krista had felt neglected and unloved at home and was unable to trust other adults in case they left her. Her teacher had engaged in a process that Allan Schore (2003) called right-brain to right-brain communication, an attachment-based, emotion-focused technique that activates and re-wires unhealthy, unconscious patterns processed and stored in the right hemisphere of the brain. Through her experiences with a teacher that would not push her away and accepted her as and where she was, Krista began to develop new pathways in her brain that allowed her to see adults and relationships in a new way. Any relationship or experience that can enrich the capacity for connection can provide "re-wiring" for our brains. As Cozolino would say, relationships become our biological structure.

Early nurturance leads to the optimal development of our brain systems and allows us to think positively about ourselves and those around us, to trust others, to regulate our emotions and behavior, and to adapt to unusual situations through problem solving. When children are abused or neglected, their brains develop in ways that do not necessarily encourage emotions and behaviors that are consistent with positive social survival. They often appear to have difficulty successfully navigating relationships or controlling their aggressive impulses because their brains see the world as a potentially threatening place where their memories tell them that they are not important or even welcome. Because development across the lifespan is fluid, memories are subject to continuously changing experiences. Relationship interactions change the structure of the brain and the brain adapts accordingly because it is designed to transform to meet the needs of the world around it.

Culture Shapes Our Experiences

Culture is a "complex, dynamic, and fascinating phenomenon. Any attempt to reduce it to a definable labeled construct demystifies that which is indeed mystic in the first place" (Matsumoto, 1996, p.11). To assist in providing some structure to represent the concept of culture, it might be helpful to conceive of "it" as a tool that defines common and shared universal beliefs, values, and behaviors that are unique to a particular group. This commonality provides some degree of personal and interpersonal meaning transmitted from generation to generation (Kagawa-Singer & Chung, 1994).

Journalist Steven Johnson writes, "The brain is the beginning of human culture, which makes culture an outgrowth of the brain's biology" (2004, p. 214). The culture into which we are born will affect how we see the world. It also affects how we see ourselves fitting into the world around us. We are influenced in a negative or positive manner by the culture of our environment. We learn to cope in our ecology, using the same coping mechanism we see modeled by others. These role models (friends and family primarily) provide cues that help us to see how we should act to be accepted by the larger community in which we live. Cultural ceremonies, rituals, and symbols are very important to us because they are part of the experiences we understand. They are a sign of comfort, stability, and familiarity. They are representative of those things and people we associate with the most and assist in the social connection process that is so vital to our brain. Where you grow up, and whom you grow up with can have a big impact on how you behave and even how your brain works. Culture exerts a significant influence on our social interactions and development.

The ways we interact with others, perceive others, and work with others are all influenced by the culture in which we live.

In *Brain and Culture*, Bruce Wexler's (2006) references one sociologist's unique interpretation on how culture shapes even something as simple as what we eat.

> Americans eat oysters but not snails. The French eat snails but not locusts. The Zulus eat locusts but not fish. The Jews eat fish but not pork. The Hindus eat pork but not beef. The Russians eat beef but not snakes. The Chinese eat snakes but not people. The Jali of New Guinea find people delicious. (p.186-187)

We know that between birth and early adulthood, the brain requires relational and experiential stimulation to develop and grow. The nature of these relationships and experiences shapes and creates the neural pathways necessary for thought and behavior. According to Wexler, a professor of psychiatry at Yale Medical School and director of the Neurocognitive Research Laboratory at the Connecticut Mental Health Center, by changing the cultural environment, each generation shapes the brains of the next (2006). The human brain creates its pathways by the experiences and relationships that stimulate it. While all experiences and relationships are important to its development, familial experiences and relationships have a greater impact on brain development and function. In the early years, adults provide surrogate brains for their offspring. These surrogate brains provide frontal lobe functions (problem-solving, decision making, even memory) that the child is not capable of. By the time they reach adolescence, their brain development allows them more control over their world and they are busy integrating experiences and relationships from many sources into a functional self (2006). This functional self becomes expressed in their actions in the world as adults, impacting their ecology and altering their environment and promoting social changes in others' capabilities and brain structure.

According to psychologists Batja Mesquita and Phoebe Ellsworth (2001), the way that we look at the world, or appraise it, may be influenced significantly by the enrichment of certain culturally based emotions. These differences frequently reflect differences in the accessibility of how we appraise and ultimately react to people and the environment. Cultural experiences not only shape our brains, they can change them as well.

Key Terms - Chapter 1

abuse	motivation	scaffolding
attunement	NeuroDynamic intervention	surrogate brain
ecological funnel	neuroplasticity	transformation
empathy	relational reimbursement	trust trials
experiential mosaic	resilience	

CHAPTER 2
Brain Wisdom

*More may have been learned about the brain and the
mind in the 1990s — the so-called decade of the brain
— than during the entire previous history of psychology
and neuroscience.*
Antonio R. Damasio

The Brain - An Organ of Adaptation

The human brain is an incredibly powerful and amazing organ. Trying
to imagine its potential is almost unfathomable. Given these statements,
it is important to note that there are basic bits of knowledge that are
critical for therapeutic helpers to know and understand that will make
them "brain wise" as they work with troubled young people. Bit by bit,
moment by moment, a youth's brain has been shaped by prior experience
and it has learned to react to what happens in today's world according
to those experiences. With over half of the human genome (a full set of
chromosomes; all of our inheritable traits) responsible for producing the
brain, it is important to understand the role it plays in the overall human
experience. Nothing even comes close to being as powerful and potential-
laden as this unique organ of adaptation. The brain is fragile, with a
consistency similar to butter, and weighs approximately three pounds. It
contains approximately 10 billion neurons with each having an axon with
dendrites that branch outward in an attempt to make connections with
approximately 60,000 to 100,000 other neurons (Edelman & Tononi,
2000). With those numbers, imagine the realm of human possibility,

combining the potential of all of the neurons and all their connections. There is an almost infinite potential available to the human species, most of which remains untapped.

Neuroplasticity – Brains of Hope

During the last three decades, a window has opened on the human brain that reveals something far more hopeful and amazing than was formerly imagined to be possible. Our brains are the only biological system in our bodies that continually attune to, and become influenced by, the internal states of those around us. In fact, our social interactions play a role in reshaping our brain through a process known as "neuroplasticity" (Goleman, 2006).

Our brain consists of neurons (nerve cells) that are interconnected and create neural pathways, a kind of superhighway for the cells. When we think, act, or experience, substantial changes occur in the shaping of these pathways by adding or removing connections and by the formation of new cells. According to the theory of neuroplasticity, experience can actually change both the brain's physical structure (anatomy) and function (physiology) throughout the brain (Doidge, brain's physical structure (anatomy) and function (physiology) throughout the brain. (Doidge, 2007).

Periods of Opportunity

All relationships and experiences, particularly early ones, directly influence the architecture of our brains. At birth, all essential structures in the brain are present. However, not all parts of the brain mature at the same time. There is an explosion of brain growth between birth and two years of age, resulting in an over-production of neural pathways followed by a selective elimination of pathways that are not used. This neural pruning, or apoptosis, is normal and necessary. The process of building and tearing down is based on the "use it or lose it" principle and allows the brain to adapt to the needs of its environment (Greenough, Black, & Wallace, 1987). Plasticity can be "additive", reinforcing existing pathways or even creating new ones, or "subtractive", a loss of pathways that are not being used. Because of the rapid brain development in children, their brains are more plastic and therefore more malleable than adults.

The fact that repeated experiences can sculpt and re-sculpt the shape, size, and number of neurons and their connections has both advantages and disadvantages. In emotionally impoverished environments, abuse and neglect can result in long-term impairment to the relationship pathways that develop in a part of the brain called the orbitofrontal cortex (Schore, 1994). We know that environmental influences and experiences early in development are able to shape neural circuits. It has been understood for years that epigenetic changes determine the long-term impact of early-life experiences. Recent studies, however, suggest that acquired epigenetic alterations, whether environmental or inherited, may be potentially reversible even after the developmental periods of sensitivity (Weaver et al., 2006). Nurturing relationships later in life can re-write and repair the missing neural connections. The brains of youth will react and adapt to new and better environments, increasing their chances for adaptivity and survival.

What's in a Brain?

The brain can be divided into four sections, which are known as lobes: the frontal lobe, parietal lobe, temporal lobe, and occipital lobe.

Frontal Lobe

The frontal lobe is located at the front of the brain and is associated with conscious thought. It enables us to maintain a simultaneous sense of self and others that is necessary for interpersonal strategizing and decision-making. The motor cortex is found at the back of the frontal lobe. This area of the brain receives information from various parts of the brain and uses this information to carry out body movements.

Parietal Lobe

The parietal lobe is located in the middle section of the brain and plays an important role in integrating information from various senses, and in the manipulation of objects. Parts of the parietal lobe are involved in visual-spatial processing. A portion of the brain known as the somatosensory cortex is located in this lobe and is essential to the processing of the body's senses.

Temporal Lobe

The temporal lobe is located in the bottom section of the brain. This lobe is important for interpreting sounds and the language we hear, as well as the processing of complex stimuli like faces and scenes. The hippocampus is also located in the temporal lobe, which is why this portion of the brain is also heavily associated with the formation of memories.

Occipital Lobe

The occipital lobe is located at the back portion of the brain and is associated with interpreting visual stimuli and information. The visual cortex, which receives and interprets information from the eyes, is located in the occipital lobe.

The Hemispheres

To physically look at the brain, one would find two distinct divisions split down the middle into a right hemisphere and a left hemisphere. These hemispheres communicate with each other through a thick band of an amazing 200–250 million nerve fibers called the corpus callosum, along with smaller bands of fibers called commissures. While the hemispheres are similar — what one side has so does the other - they also have areas of specialization. Each hemisphere appears to be specialized for some behaviors and functions and has developed to perceive life experiences quite uniquely.

Left and Right Brain Functions

Left Brain Functions

Logic Linear

Digital **System**

Objective

Analytic thought Novel

Color

Verbal **Order**

Art and music

Language Dream **Emotion**

Science and math **Intuition** **Big**

Free

Logical Random

Imagination Creativity

Holistic thought

Creative

Right Brain Functions

The primary duty of the right side of the brain is to control muscles on the left side of the body, and the left side of the brain controls muscles on the right side of the body. Also, in general, sensory information from the left side of the body crosses over to the right side of the brain and information from the right side of the body crosses over to the left side of the brain.

Left Hemisphere

In humans, the left hemisphere is usually the dominant one of the two, and is biased towards analytical and sequential thinking. While both hemispheres are responsible for aspects of language function, most of the specialized language areas are found in the left hemisphere. The left hemisphere is dominant for instructing us how to consciously cope and problem solve. It focuses and elaborates on detail by incorporating logic and concreteness into our thinking patterns. The left hemisphere is critical in helping to produce explanations of our experiences by decoding details and organizing them into understandable events. When we are able to make sense of the events that take place in our lives, we are able to predict and plan more effectively and efficiently. The left hemisphere appears to be associated with details and information.

Right Hemisphere

The right hemisphere is biased in the control of emotion, bodily experience, and processes that are out of our voluntary control (Devinsky, 2000). It specializes in receiving and analyzing information from the outside world, especially those social cues received from the verbal and non-verbal behavior of others. It appraises safety and danger, helping us to decide whether to approach or avoid specific individuals and situations. The right hemisphere also appears to be dominant for facial recognition, visual imagery, body awareness, and socio-emotional information. The right hemisphere provides a more global perspective, helping us to make sense of ourselves, those around us and our social relationships. The right hemisphere helps us connect how we "feel" about our life experiences and guides us in our decision-making, especially those things that we might want to avoid in life.

People Need People to Heal

Healthy brains are integrated brains. Integration occurs when the left and right hemispheres are working in collaboration with each other and information is being exchanged efficiently between both hemispheres through the corpus callosum. This coordination of the hemispheres appears to be stimulated when we attune well with others, particularly in the first few years of life. The integration of the hemispheres allows us to be flexible in how we think and self-regulate our behavior. (Badenoch, 2008, Siegel, 2007). Failure to connect and attune with others tends to lead to rigid and or chaotic ways of thinking. When therapeutic helpers are acting in a therapeutic way, they are attuning by connecting with challenging youth via their right brains. In essence, connection takes place in and between people's right hemispheres. Since the right brain assists us in understanding our personal stories, the left brain adds the needed details to make sense of the various experiences since birth. These experiences have shaped the neural structures within the brain and have resulted in the design of specific behavioral patterns that have adapted to the people and world around them. When the hemispheres of the brains of youth are not integrated, they are heavily influenced by one hemisphere and become stuck and unable to see multiple perspectives. They may become overly reliant upon strategies that do not work, yet they keep using them over and over. Life might be experienced as too rigid and concrete (left hemisphere) or too uncertain, disorganized or unpredictable (right brain). Proper integration is crucial in the healing process. Therapeutic helpers must use their left-brain to identify strategies and supports that will help the youth while accessing their right brains to connect and relate to them in a meaningful and genuine manner.

How the Brain Builds Itself

The human brain builds itself based upon the way it is used in life, from the bottom up and from the back to the front. It develops from the least complex to the most complex areas. While significantly interconnected, each of the regions of the brain mediates distinct functions. At birth, the brainstem areas responsible for regulating cardiovascular and respiratory function must be intact for the infant to survive. This must be organized in utero.

Bottom to Top and Back to Front

After the brainstem, the midbrain develops. This area focuses on survival functions such as safety and threat response. Next in the developmental order is the limbic area that deals primarily with our feelings and emotions. The largest and the last parts of the brain to develop are the frontal lobes and sections of the brain that provide the ability to reason, plan, anticipate, and predict. These parts of the brain develop most rapidly during adolescence and early adulthood.

As the brain is developing from bottom to top this process is influenced by a host of neurotransmitters, neurohormones, and neuromodulator signals. These signals help target cells to migrate, differentiate, and form connections. These crucial neural networks originate in the lower brain areas and project to every other part of the developing brain. This allows these systems the unique capacity to communicate across multiple regions simultaneously and therefore provide an organizing and orchestrating role during development later in life.

Right then Left

The right hemisphere develops first and grows quite rapidly during the first 18 months of life. This coincides with the development of sensory and motor capabilities that go hand-in-hand, matching our relational and ecological experiences. At the same time, the basic structures of attachment and emotional regulation are being established in the right side of the frontal lobe, while the development of the left hemisphere is slowed (Schore, 1994). During the second year of life, the left hemisphere has a growth spurt as babies learn to move about their world. The focus of the frontal lobes shifts to learning of language and eye-hand coordination. The corpus callosum, the bundle of neural fibers that connect the hemispheres, begins to develop near the end of the first year. This allows for the integration of the hemispheres' capabilities, although alternating growth spurts occur generally in the hemispheres until the age of 12.

The Adolescent Brain - From Here to Maturity

In adults, various parts of the brain work together to evaluate choices, make decisions, and act accordingly in each situation. A young person's brain doesn't appear to work this way. One reason is that the prefrontal cortex is always a work in progress. The primary part of the logical brain that helps adults make good decisions is immature and under-developed in teenagers. In fact, it may not fully develop and mature until the mid-20s or later. In addition, teenagers experience a wealth of growth in synapses during adolescence. Following the boom, just as happens in the earlier remodeling periods, the brain starts pruning away the synapses that it doesn't need in order to make the remaining ones more efficient in communicating. In humans, this maturation process starts in the back of the brain and moves forward, so that the prefrontal cortex, that vital center of control, is the last to be pruned and mature.

Metacognition

This means that, oftentimes because the pre-frontal cortex is not fully developed, teenagers are not using the part of their brains that plays an essential role in impulse control, decision-making, planning, and prediction. Adult brains are also better wired to notice errors in decision-making and pick up on them more quickly. This comes from a more mature frontal lobe that is used more extensively. It also comes from an ability that comes with brain maturity - metacognition. Metacognition is the ability to think about your thinking. It is a process that requires self-monitoring, self-representation, and self-regulation processes, which are regarded as integral components of the mature human mind. These capacities are used to regulate one's own thinking and to maximize one's potential to think. This ability comes after that massive neural pruning that comes in adolescence. While it may sound counter-intuitive, synaptic connections and neurons that have not been used enough waste a great deal of blood, oxygen, and energy. Pruning them out keeps the brain focused and efficient (Doidge, 2007).

Apoptosis

Until that pruning and rewiring are complete, teenagers and young adults tend to perform cognitive tasks (make decisions, problem-solve, and predict the future) largely in their temporal lobes; the shift to the frontal lobes does not happen until later in life, regardless of level of education (Springer, McIntosh, Wincour, & Grady, 2005). This processing shift within the brain is another example of plasticity. Often, we ask young people to elicit their metacognitive awareness before they have acquired maturity and proficiency in this area, in essence, asking them to do something that any are not yet developmentally capable of doing.

The frontal lobes, or what Daniel Goleman (1998) calls the "just say no" section of the brain, may not be fully mature and functional until the early to mid-twenties, but one area of the teenager's brain that is fairly well developed early on is the nucleus accumbens, the part of the brain that seeks pleasure and reward. Studies using imaging techniques compared brain activity when receiving a small, medium, or large reward. Teenagers exhibited exaggerated responses to medium and large rewards compared to children and adults. The teenagers' brains showed minimal activity when presented with a small reward in comparison to adults' and children's brains (Powell, 2006).

Youth with immature decision-making capabilities and a strong desire for reward can appear to display rebellious, risk-taking behavior and increased potential addiction issues. However, all the news is not bad. During this time, the brain is acting a bit like a sponge; it can soak up new information and change to make room for it. The increased growth and neural pruning increases plasticity and plasticity can help these young people pick up new skills and build new neural pathways through better and positive experiences. This is an opportune time for therapeutic helpers to be with, feel with, and go with youth in an attempt to re-sculpt experience.

The Triune Brain – Three Brains in One

For simplicity, we will limit the majority of our descriptions of the brain to follow the framework set forward in the 1980s by neurologist Paul MacLean. He believes that the brain operates like three interconnected biological components, each with its own special intelligence, its own subjectivity, its own sense of time and space, and its own memory: the reptilian or survival brain, the emotional or mammalian brain, and the thinking/logical brain, or neocortex. He identifies these "brains" as being connected, yet operating with separate capacities.

James E. Zull (2002) states that it is important to return to our biological roots to understand how our brain shares common "wants." Simply put, the brain wants to survive and survive well. The combination of the components of the brain is designed to act as a very comprehensive survival machine. We take in sensory data from our environment, integrate it, and ultimately act upon what we experience to make the best of life.

The Reptilian Brain

Believe it or not, we are all a little bit reptilian. Each of us has a part of the brain that dates back to the times when reptiles most likely ruled the earth. The reptilian brain was formed long before humans began to take shape. Sitting as the crown jewel of the spine and at the base of the skull, it plays a variety of roles in the regulation of basic life functions. Although we have grown and transformed our human abilities into more advanced and intricate ways of surviving this journey called life, we have managed to maintain certain primitive abilities along the way that play a collaborative role with the other brain systems in helping us to survive.

As the oldest part of our brain, the reptilian brain is responsible for the vital functions of our overall physiological survival. This brain regulates our sleep/wake cycle, heart rate, respiration, balance, and overall body temperature. Our basic reproductive impulse is anchored here, along with our sense of environmental protectiveness, our sensory-motor reactions, and the startle reflex.

The reptilian brain relies heavily upon sensory information from the outside world to help respond internally to the various scenarios that take place in our ecologies. It concerns itself with what is happening now, not in the future. It is detail-oriented and doesn't have the ability to reflect on its reactions. The reptilian brain is instinctual and therefore just reacts. It does not think.

Since humans have a fairly long history of experiencing life on Earth, opportunities have been afforded to us to learn about the various situations that could be labeled as either safe or dangerous. Over time, these experiences have played a significant role in shaping who we have become and have helped us to fine-tune this brain sector to be ever alert to potential threats or harm. The brain attunes itself to the clues that are fed to the reptilian sector that tell us when to approach someone in a crowded room or when to avoid a dangerous animal we meet while on a leisurely walk. The reptilian brain is all about keeping us alive and well. The famous fight, flight, and freeze behavioral reactions are protective factors within the reptilian brain and keep us safe when we have no time to think because thinking could mean loss of time and loss of time could potentially mean death. These are similar features we commonly share with snakes, lizards, iguanas, and other similar animals that have a "strike first – never ask questions" mentality.

The reptilian brain is always scanning for danger. It is a quick responder to potential threats and the relationship the perceived threat has had to the experiences of our ancestors and those in our own personal lives. In a sense, our reactions are rooted in our genetics and experiences. Based upon our own personal experiences, certain sights, sounds, tastes, touches and smells may evoke a reactive response. The reptilian brain has often been described as being rigid and reactive, with a hint of paranoia. Filled with ancestral memories, we are reactively guided by our past and present by this primitive brain system.

The Emotional Brain

The emotional brain or limbic system, as it is frequently known, is the primary seat of emotion. It appears to be very dedicated to the cultivation of emotional experience and its association with experiential memory, including those experiences that include the good, the bad, and the downright ugly. It is involved in primal activities related to food and sex, particularly having to do with our sense of smell and bonding needs, and activities related to expression and mediation of emotions and feelings, including emotions linked to attachment.

This association assists humans in supporting decisions made in the "thinking" systems based upon emotional experience. The emotional brain is a complex set of structures that lie on both sides of the thalamus, directly above the cerebrum. As neurologist David Kolb states, "True learning, learning for real comprehension, comes through a sequence of experience, reflection, abstraction and active testing" (1984). Generally speaking, reference to the emotional system includes the amygdala, hippocampus, hypothalamus, and the pituitary. Each of these areas is uniquely involved in the expression and assimilation of emotionally evoked scenarios.

Amygdala

The amygdala is an almond-sized and shaped structure located deep in the medial temporal lobe (you actually have two — one in each hemisphere of the brain). It is essential for us to have the ability to feel certain emotions and to perceive them in other people. This includes fear and the many changes that it causes in the body. If, for example, you are being followed at night by a shady-looking character, you are afraid, and your heart is pounding, chances are that your amygdala is very active.

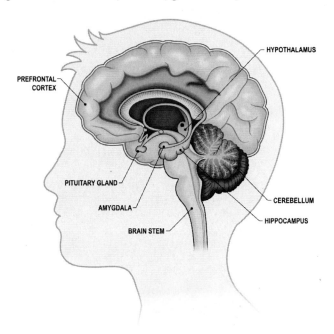

The amygdala modulates all of our reactions to events that are important for our survival. Events that warn us of imminent danger are therefore very important stimuli for the amygdala, as are events that signal the presence of food, sexual partners, and competition. The amygdala plays a protective role by letting us react almost instantaneously to the presence of danger. This reaction happens so quickly that we often startle first, and only afterwards are aware of what it was that frightened us.

A friend tells a story of growing up in a household with an alcoholic father who was prone to anger and violence when under the influence. When drunk, which was frequently, his father would beat him for mostly random and unknown reasons. Just before he set upon him, he would reach for his belt, giving my friend just enough time to realize the impending pain that he was about to endure. To this day, he says all he has to see is someone put his hand to his waist and he feels panic and the urge to run. His reptilian brain is rooted in this negative childhood experience and he reacts without thought. This type of memory was maintained by the brain to be used in the future to "trigger" the perception of potential danger. In his case, his experiences with belts were so painful that his brain now prepares itself for pain just by seeing familiar actions; a simple movement of a hand to the belt is all it takes to evoke emergency action.

Compare that with the childhood experiences of another friend. He grew up in a large, close-knit farm family that spent the majority of its family time in the kitchen. The older children did homework at the kitchen table while the younger siblings played nearby on the floor. His mother and grandmother cooked for the family and the farmhands, and the smell of coffee and fresh baking was always wafting through the kitchen. He has been working in the city in a stressful job for many years, but the smells from a bakery or coffee shop still evoke great feelings of happiness and contentment, even in the middle of a very difficult day. His reptilian brain is rooted in a very different and positive experience, but evokes just as strong a reaction in his body.

The brain is sufficiently powerful that it can bring forth both good and bad emotional reactions to people and experiences. When in healthy balance, both have been helpful in not only surviving, but also surviving well.

Amygdala War

Many times the young people we work with are filled with prior experiences that have been threatening or actually involved issues of survival. Therefore, they may be overly sensitive to the day-to-day events that most of us take for granted. Because of this sensitivity, they are often quick to engage in powerful survival strategies that have been historically useful in stopping others or situations from becoming a problem. Their amygdala remains in an over-active state and makes them prone to over-reacting behavior (overt aggression, passive aggression, yelling, violently posturing etc.) These are attempts to divert real or perceived threat. If these types of behavior do not result in diversion of the perceived threat or make the adult involved go away, these young people will then resort to engaging them by arguing and fighting with them. When this type of engagement occurs with another person, we have what our NeuroTransactional model terms an amygdala war.

This takes place when two people become entangled with one another and their two survival systems are actively "fighting," one trying to overpower the other and reduce the threat. These engagements are counter-productive because they are simply utilizing the most primitive systems in our brain. These systems only react. No thinking is taking place. When we have two reactive individuals, we have two non-thinking individuals who set the stage for a powerfully negative outcome. Therapeutic helpers trained in our model will recognize the early signs of a youth attempting to engage in an amygdala war and will utilize their own logical /cognitive strength to diffuse and deflect the engagement.

As discussed in the section in Chapter 1 on NeuroDynamic Interventions (NDIs), NDIs are knowledge and skills that therapeutic helpers use "in the moment" to effectively work with the youth's brain state. To avoid an amygdala war, the therapeutic helper uses an NDI, their knowledge of the non-thinking reactiveness of the amygdala, to avoid becoming counter-aggressive and reactive themselves. In the story that follows, consider the actions taken by Tanya's worker and how using an NDI could have changed the damage to the relationship for both Tanya and her worker.

Story - Tanya and the Shoes

Tanya was a 14-year-old group home resident. She had a history of oppositional behavior and struggled with the rules of the home. One cold winter evening after dinner, Tanya decided she was going out to meet her friends at the local mall instead of joining the others in the common room to do homework. As she prepared to go, her worker came up to her and told her that it was homework time and that she was not to leave the building. Tanya responded by swearing at the worker, saying that she was going out and no one was going to stop her. The worker took umbrage with the language and the defiance and told Tanya that she, in fact, was going to stop her. Tanya shoved her and told her to get the *&!% out of her way. The worker grabbed Tanya's shoes and taunted her, telling her she was going nowhere because she had her shoes. The taunting infuriated Tanya and she started screaming and threatening the worker. She grabbed her hair and pulled hard, trying to get her to drop the shoes. The worker returned the reactive behavior by grabbing and pulling Tanya's hair. The commotion brought other workers to the scene where Tanya and the worker were struggling in a heap on the floor. Tanya was restrained, kicking, screaming, and crying. She was put on restriction for a month - only able to leave her room to be accompanied to classes.

Why Reactive Strategies Rarely Work

Reactive behavioral approaches, like the incident with Tanya make bad NeuroTransactional sense. The brain systems involved with basic punishment and initial pain are primitive and any animal can feel the impact of pain. Humans are unique in that they have a highly evolved logical system that can work through the challenges given to us by life. Using primitive strategies to change behavior is primitive in and of itself. Wise adults utilize the brain's ability to think and decide to guide youth to logical choice that will serve them well in the moment and later in life. Reducing the human experience to a primitive level will only breed a primitive response from youth. This will ensure both the youth and the adult demonstrate a cycle of non-thinking reactive behavior rooted in our most primitive of interactions.

The Hippocampus

The hippocampus is a horseshoe-shaped structure adjacent to the amygdala. Like the amygdala, the hippocampus is a paired structure with mirror-image halves in the left and right sides of the brain. The hippocampus has several functions, but one of its most important seems to be its role in the formation of new memories about experiences in life. Research into the role of the hippocampus suggests that during wakefulness the hippocampus receives input from other parts of the brain involved in the initial encoding of an experience and binds this information into a memory. This memory is then transferred to the neocortex during sleep where it is stored and integrated within pre-existing memories. This process can take up to a year or more. While some memory transfer occurs when we are awake, most happens largely during sleep, where the hippocampus "replays" the bits and pieces of the experience, embedding them deeper and deeper into the brain until they are more or less permanent (Carter, 1998). Until this happens, the hippocampus is needed to retrieve and put that memory in the context of the different bit and pieces of the memory until it is fully encoded or stored. The hippocampus also assesses experiences to determine if they are threatening or neutral. If the hippocampus perceives the experience as neutral, it sends a message to the amygdala to stop the stress response (LeDoux, 1996, Van der Kolk, 1996). The hippocampus is very susceptible to the chemicals produced when stress or threat is perceived.

Hormones

In addition to the emotional brain being our source of our urges, desires, and emotions, it also allows for the control of additional functions above and beyond those of our reptilian brain. The hypothalamus links our nervous system to our endocrine system via the pituitary gland. It synthesizes and secretes certain neurohormones (oxytocin, vasopressin, and dopamine are the most well-known) that in turn stimulate or inhibit the secretion of pituitary hormones. Oxytocin and vasopressin are "bonding hormones" that enhance connections between males and females, mothers and children, and increase the levels of trust between people in general. The hypothalamus and the amygdala often work hand in hand, sending signals back and forth. In times of danger, the amygdala sends signals to the hypothalamus that can activate the fight or flight response in the nervous system.

The pituitary gland assists in the fight or flight response as well. Once the hypothalamus initiates the nervous system to fight or flee, the pituitary gland stimulates the adrenal glands, causing them to secrete cortisol. Cortisol is a steroid hormone that helps the body by converting fats to sugars and inhibiting the immune response, giving it the needed burst of energy in a survival situation. Intended as a short-term response, in a chronic state, cortisol can impair the stress response, making it more reactive and less adaptive.

Beyond Fight or Flight

Neuroscientists use the amygdala response - the fight or flight reflex - to explain how our brains process fear by reacting instantaneously and without conscious thought to present and immediate threat. However, most of the young people that we work with spend a great deal of time dealing with fear of ambiguous situations and general uncertainty. Past experiences have made them leery of adults in positions of authority. There may not be a clear and present threat but their past experiences can create a state of hypervigilance in their risk assessment of their environment.

Recent research is showing that another part of the brain close to the amygdala, the bed nucleus of the stria terminalis (BNST), has a key role in processing ambiguous and uncertain threats (LeDoux, 2015). Like the amygdala, it connects with the hippocampus, the prefrontal cortex, and other brain circuits and can exhibit amygdala like behaviors like flight or freezing, but the BNST becomes active when we are anxious about unpredictable situations. This activation is in addition to the amygdala and can extend hypervigilance and negative emotional regulation and responses (Alverez et al., 2011). While there is much more research required, neuroscientists believe that this information may lead to a change in the way we understand emotional regulation and anxiety disorders (Knight & Dupue, 2019).

The Emotional World

What is an emotion, or better yet, what is "in" an emotion? For thousands of years, attempts to define the word "emotion" have resulted in numerous interpretations of the word, ranging from the simplest to the most complex.

Even today, as modern technology begins to play an ever-increasing role in providing us with greater insight into the emotional realm of our brain, one thing is certain. No matter the definition of the word, we cannot separate emotion from our daily routine; in fact, it is impossible to take the emotion out of our life.

As humans, we are an emotional species and emotions come naturally to us whether we like it or not. They have played, and will continue to play, a significant role in our lives. According to John Ratey (2001), clinical professor at Harvard Medical School, "We are learning that emotions are a result of multiple brain and body systems that are distributed over the whole person. We cannot separate emotion from cognition or cognition from the body" (p. 223). He further states that this new belief in emotion is counter to previous thinking that compartmentalized emotion to a specific area of the brain. "Emotion is messy, complicated, primitive, and undefined because it is all over the place, intertwined with cognition and physiology" (p. 223). In essence, we are stuck with emotions and that can be either a good or bad thing, dependent upon our genetic blueprint along with our environmental and relational experiences.

Over the course of time, emotions have been an instrumental force in our overall survival, as they have played a pivotal role in our endurance and superiority as a species. Emotions have adapted to allow us to change along with the world around us. Charles Darwin took a functional approach by proposing that emotions can be conceived as avenues towards flexible adaptation, which prepare appropriate responses that can be utilized rapidly (such as freezing in fear) and goal-directed behavior strategies (such as attack, avoidance, or proximity-seeking) for dealing with both crises and opportunity (Roseman,1984; Scherer, 2000).

Emotions Add "Spice" to Memory

Emotions are states that are created within our bodies based upon the information and experiences we receive from the outside world. Even moments of contemplation are somehow evoked from an external stimulus. When we hear, see, taste, touch, or smell something, our brains react by sending the bits and pieces of this sensory information to the appropriate areas of the brain as memories. Emotions assist our memory systems by adding "spice" so that each memory has a particular flavor and strength to it, creating emotional templates that are stored for later use. When we experience similar stimuli, the body then behaves based on the direction it receives from that particular emotional "template" generated by the limbic system. It is through these templates that were shaped by prior experiences that our body collaborates with the brain to create the recipe for displaying emotion through, what is commonly referred to as, behavior.

Psychologists Paul Ekman and Richard Davidson (1994) believe that emotions provide events with salience. With increased experience and social success, people begin to see relevance in their interactions and are able to fine-tune their expressions of emotion to better fit the ecologies in which they live. Within the brain, this is accomplished through the development of networks that connect thinking and feeling, cognitive-affective networks. Neuroscientist Joseph LeDoux, (1996) indicates that there are different classes of emotional behavior that "represent different kinds of functions that take care of different kinds of problems and different brain systems devoted to them" (p.127).

Emotions as Communication

People are born ready to experience a full range of emotions. Our brains expect that normal development will include varying degrees of good and bad, as well as the spectrum of experiences that may fall in between the two. To achieve a balanced emotional life, one that is filled with pro-adaptivity, happiness, and optimal functioning, we must be able to recognize our emotions, regulate them, and alter them as our relationships and ecologies require.

Emotions are quite simple in design, but complex in all that it takes to put one into action. When we receive sad news, our brain interprets the sad components of the event and the emotional system then tells the body to move or "behave" in a sad way and, as a result, people see us looking or acting sad (frowning faces, withdrawal, etc.). Conversely, when we are told happy news, our brain tells the body to move or behave in happy ways and people see us displaying happiness through our behavior (smiling, laughing, etc.). In many cases, our emotions are clearly interpretable just from our facial expressions.

It is through this display of emotion that we communicate our internal states to those around us. Without the external display of emotion, we would be hard to interpret and interact with as a species. People would not be able to readily and efficiently respond to our needs, as we would simply just "be." Relying upon the emotional behavior of others to tell us how they are feeling on the inside helps us to take notice of their needs and respond appropriately. When we are aware of the needs of others, we can be more caring, supportive, and compassionate. Emotions help us maintain connections to the past so that our present and future actions are more informed. Neuroscientist and psychobiologist Jaak Panksepp (1998), a noted researcher on emotions, states that an intensely caring and generous attitude known as altruism plays a critical role in the expansion of the human brain. We have survived by sticking together, realizing someone needs help, and coming to his or her aid, but with just enough aid to be generous and not overwhelming. Generosity thrives in a state of balance by facilitating cooperation, sharing, and communication.

During the course of our daily routines, events capture our attention and based on their level of importance are stamped within an appropriate emotional memory system. Once stamped and sorted, the various bits and pieces of data are stored in just the right places for future access. The bits and pieces stand ready to be reassembled in future experiences. When something, someone, or an event stimulates an emotional template, or "response recipe," the result is some sort of action based upon prior experiences. These automatic bodily reactions occur unconsciously and rapidly. In many cases, an emotion lasts only for seconds and may involve a variety of stress responses, facial expressions, and body language. It is important to remember that emotion is a brain-body experience.

Currently, four primary emotions appear to be accepted by most present day researchers — fear, anger, sadness, and joy. Each of the emotions has "sub-emotions" (fear-anxiety, anger-frustration, sadness-depression, joy-exhilaration, and so on). Simply put, it is believed that from these basic emotions come all others. However, Paul Ekman and Richard Davidson (1994) go on to further propose that within that emotional spectrum, there are six specific universal emotions that humans display across cultures; these emotions, surprise, happiness, anger, fear, disgust, and sadness, are standard and reliable despite where a person might live, the language spoken, or the degree of education attained. These standard emotions help to facilitate communication between the individual's mind and body, and ultimately between the minds and bodies of others. This interaction encourages the organization of how we take in the world around us, think about our approach to life, recall memories of past experiences, move our body in certain ways, and relate to others by displaying certain behaviors.

Appraisal and Response

Appraisal is essential to accurate and effective emotional processing. When the brain appraises, it is scanning the self and the ecology by evaluating the multitudes of bits and pieces of the world around it for some type of emotional meaning or relevance. We cannot remove emotion from our existence, so we are always scanning to produce meaning from our internal and external worlds. We will only present the amygdala and orbitofrontal cortex as the two major players in the emotional appraisal process. Although other parts of the brain contribute to the appraisal process, these are the critical neural areas involved in functional appraisal.

At a basic level, what we take in from our external or internal worlds can be either positive or negative. Positive stimuli might include seeing someone smile after receiving a gift, finding a check for a million dollars with your name on it, or identifying a picture of a lost child on the side of a milk carton. Negative stimuli might be experiencing pain from the harsh words of another person, seeing a suspicious person standing next to your car at a mall parking lot, or watching a child being verbally hurt by an adult.

When either the amygdala (located deep within the brain) or the orbitofrontal cortex (located in front section of the brain) receives stimuli that are perceived to be relevant, they send information to the hypothalamus and brainstem. This initiates the appropriate emotional response to be carried out by the brain and body as well as the release of appropriate hormones, autonomic nervous system responses, and movement by the person's musculoskeletal system.

Critical to the efficient processing of emotional situations, the hypothalamus provides specific support through the regulation of our hormones. Hormones are chemical regulators. Of particular interest is the regulation of cortisol levels through the hypothalamus-pituitary-adrenal axis (HPA). The hypothalamus encourages the pituitary to produce endorphins, natural pain relievers, and oxytocin or vasopressin that are bonding hormones essential to our social attachment system. Consider the importance of this process when two people are interacting. Both persons' brains and bodies are actually engaging in a hormonal dance of mutual regulation, when one is creating a particular state in the other and vice versa. When the regulation is "good enough" between the people, the interaction is successful between their brains and bodies. This would be considered a positive outcome.

The autonomic system is controlled jointly by the hypothalamus and brainstem. The autonomic system is a regulatory branch of the central nervous system that helps people adapt to changes in their environment. The autonomic system is further divided into the sympathetic and parasympathetic nervous system. The sympathetic system regulates actions taken in response to what happens in the outside ecology and stands ready to implement such behavior as fight, flight, or freezing to protect us from impending danger. The parasympathetic system nurtures our internal system by aiding in processes such as repair and balance. Working together, the sympathetic and parasympathetic nervous systems can control just how intensively we react to a stimulus.

When we produce "emotional" behavior, we are actually witnessing the hypothalamus and brainstem working together, as they control the cranial nerves and spinal cord to produce the desired emotional state. Examples of this might include the fight, flight, or freeze behavior that is initiated by something adverse or challenging to us within our ecology. Most people understand the concept of fight and flight, but freezing is just as powerful a tool used by many animal species, including humans. Freezing allows us to be less detected and provides for increased focus and attention to the challenge at hand.

Ekman (1992) states that we have good cortical control over our skeletal movement, but less control over our vocal cords and very little control over autonomic connections to our vital organs. A pioneer in the study of facial expressions and emotion, Ekman concludes that we may be able to mask our facial expressions of emotion, but are less likely to hide a trembling voice or the "red face" that an embarrassing moment might cause. We are in control of some of our body reactions, but others are out of our control and can give us away in challenging situations.

The body and brain have a transactional relationship with experiences in life. In most cases, transactions with brain, body, and everyday experiences occur unconsciously. At first, not utilizing a conscious state most of the time might sound a little unusual. However, it is one of the amazing protective abilities our brain possesses as part of its overall neural conservation program. Our brains selectively identify what is critical to consciousness and what is not based on how much energy or resources it must expend on a given task. If your brain had to consciously account for every piece of information that it took in, every step and every breath you took, it would be overwhelmed and result in a "neural superhighway traffic jam."

Moved by Emotion

We use emotion to move us in a particular direction. Imagine times when you have been *moved to laughter* by a happy movie or *moved to tears* by a sad story. It was in those moments that you were moved by your emotion and potentially the emotional contagion of others. In these two examples, when you were emotionally moved by an experience, others observed your inside emotional state by the outward behavior you displayed by either laughing or crying. The observers immediately made a determination about your internal feelings based upon your outward behavior. Since many of our emotional templates are so similar, we often find ourselves laughing and crying about the same things or events. In fact, we are so similar that when people around us do not respond in a similar way, we are quick to identify them as different, bizarre, creepy, or dangerous. Lack of similar emotional response by others has also served as a protective agent by alerting us to potential individuals that may not share similar historical experiences and may be dangerous to affiliate with. Dangerous affiliations decrease our chances for surviving or surviving well. As a result, we might isolate or shun challenging youth, either temporarily or permanently, until our thoughts are either confirmed or denied. This is the survival mechanism of our brain in action. Emotions have been enhanced over time to assist us in finding more adaptive solutions to problems, regulating our body, finding food, defending against danger, reproducing, caring for offspring, and maintaining social interactions (LeDoux, 1996; Pinker, 1997).

Throughout life, emotions assist us in responding appropriately to those experiences that are rewarding and those that are painful. Through a very precise and coordinated effort, emotion attempts to get a person's mind and body "in sync." This synchronicity allows for the organization of perception, cognition, memory, body movement, behavior, and interpersonal communication so that we are primed to cope with the presenting situation or event. The priming of our brain and body allows for future planning and the prediction of what might be to come, providing for the possibility that we might select the correct emotional template, resulting in just the right behavior for the circumstance. When we do this well, we are considered to be adaptive; when we do it poorly, people label us as dysfunctional, antisocial, dysregulated, or unable to cope.

Emotional Flexibility

According to neurologist Antonio Damasio, "Emotions play out in the theatre of the body. Feelings play out in the theatre of the mind" (2003, p. 28). In order for emotional responses to work well and provide a person with adaptive responses to life events, they must be flexible and able to adapt to a variety of situations and in a multitude of circumstances.

Modern day positive psychologists believe that emotional flexibility is the key to optimal functioning. People who perceive their world as positive are generally accepted by a greater number of people. Positive emotional tone or behavior promotes a sense of well-being in others and people are drawn towards this energy. Positive behavior is also very motivating; it encourages positive brain states in others. People will often state that being around a person emanating positive behavior is entrancing and they feel as if they are drawn in to being physically close to these types of people. An example of this type of power is what a good comedian might have over an audience in a comedy club. Imagine the concept of the stand-up comedy routine itself. If the performer is good it is a journey into all things funny and frequently takes the audience outside of their natural boundaries. This allows them to laugh when they otherwise might not have felt it to be socially appropriate, enduring criticism.

Feelings ...They're What We Know

Although commonly confused with emotions, feelings serve a separate function. Emotions are the bodily response recipes for behavioral action and feelings are the conscious "what we know" components about the bodily and mindful responses within our working memory. Feelings are the perceived outcome of unconscious emotional processing. Emotions are defined by bodily response, while feelings are more experiential. Imagine for a moment that you are walking down a busy sidewalk. You step into the street and a speeding motorcycle zooms by and narrowly misses you. Because your survival system took control, your heart is beating wildly, your hands are sweating profusely, and your whole body is shaking. This was an emotional response to the event that elicited behavior from the appropriate brain systems. However, if asked you how you "felt," you would be recalling the experience based on the emotional template or behavior that you displayed during and following the specific incident. You would recall the heart beating wildly, sweaty hands, and shaking. Once our conscious brain identifies what we did and how we did it, we label the situation with a "feeling" word. It helps to centralize how brain and body states join forces and eventually label the emotional reaction with a word such as "terrifying" or "scary." In this scenario, terrifying and scary are examples of the descriptive words that label how the brain and body provided an emotional reaction to a situation.

In a sense, emotions move us to action and feelings label the action. The use of feelings helps us to develop commonality among our peers, so when a person says they feel "happy" or "nervous," others recognize the word and draw from their own emotional memory in order relate to their current brain and body state. This type of social recognition increases the chance for support or nurturance, and ultimately our survival. It also sets the stage for relational care and connectedness called empathy.

The Logical Brain

The emotional brain also receives input from and can be controlled by the thinking brain. The human cerebral cortex (the logical brain) is the part of the brain at the front of our heads that sets us apart from all other animals. This part of the brain is responsible for cognition, and plays an essential role in perception, memory, thought, intellect, and consciousness. The cerebral cortex provides impulse control, decision-making, and assists in the prediction of future outcomes. It helps to modulate our emotions, body movement, and general behavior. People who have not had a normal course of development will respond differently in these areas because appropriate people have not been involved in their lives, ultimately creating the thinking systems within the brain differently than those who have had typical development.

Like an excavator used on a construction site, the cerebral cortex can "dig" into the brain and pull up information from other parts of the brain to help us make decisions by consolidating bits and pieces of information based on survival and emotional experiences in our past. However, the brain is only able to dig down and retrieve what is there. If a youth's life has been filled with stress, abuse, or trauma, the brain can only retrieve those types of memories. When a youth's life has had a more balanced experience of both good and bad, then it is has more choices in its "file cabinet of life." Having more choices means more potential outcomes. More potential outcomes provide more opportunities to have the right coping skill to apply to the scenario needing attention. Because of this unique ability, humans often seek people with more experience in certain areas of life and especially those who can put the bits and pieces together in a clear, concise, and easily understood manner to assist them during difficult times. Logical brains can be shaped by anything and anyone. So, looking at the logical approaches a youth takes towards life often tells us much about his or her experiences and what has worked or not worked

The logical brain cannot ignore emotions, but it does try to help make sense of them and learn to regulate them better in life. When we ask someone to think logically, they can only draw on their existing "files." Logic is based on experience, so what can be quite illogical to one person (if he or she is lacking experiences) can make perfect sense to someone else.

The logical brain helps guide us in understanding our past, our present, and plans for the expected future. In fact, we spend a significant portion of our lives planning for future events that are based on prior experiences. An example of this might be when one says, "I usually take the highway to get to the supermarket because it's faster." Although this is a simple statement, it exemplifies how prior experiences of trying multiple routes resulted in a decision that one particular one was a better choice over the others, thus shaping how we decide to drive to the supermarket in the future.

Our brains are designed to become aware of situations and events that need our "attention." Consciousness is an ultra-alert state that allows us to absorb more details about what is happening around us. Consciousness allows us to use our thinking brains and divert the necessary energy into areas that support thinking. Because being conscious to details requires significant energy, our brain is designed to be "energy-wise." In fact, our brain prefers to be as efficient as possible. As a result, we make a majority of life's decisions in an unconscious state, only becoming conscious when necessary.

We might drive to work one day and once we arrive at our destination find ourselves amazed at how we didn't remember anything from the drive. We might ask…did I run that red light? Did I stop at *every* stop sign? This is a perfect example of our brains operating quite successfully in an unconscious state. How the conscious and unconscious states of the brain work together is not fully understood. Some researchers speculate that the processing between the brain's hemispheres may have something to do with it. Some theorists believe that we always perceive things around us (unconsciousness) but once we can relate what we perceive to stored memory files, things that make sense to us, we become conscious. The act of relating to internal categories that we have created leads to conscious perception (Ratey, 2001). Regardless of how it actually happens, we do know that we become conscious of things when we decide to pay attention to something that we already perceive.

Another way the brain is energy-conscious is through the ability to make connections in the environment by using a "good enough" match. The brain doesn't require perfection, just a "good enough" match to establish a connection. The brain is an estimator or predictor in most daily events. Since nothing in life is exactly the same as anything else, this brain approach is helpful as we navigate through life making decisions about "what to do" in a situation and "how to" handle a problem. If the brain had to make perfect matches, the brain would exhaust itself because we live in an imperfect world. Good enough matches allow us the ability to make sufficient connections without wasting precious neural resources.

Our brains constantly and automatically process what we see, matching it to a pattern that we are familiar with, and creates a perception. When we see a four-legged animal walking towards us on the street, for example, we can identify it as a dog even if we have not seen that particular breed before. Our brains automatically generate the perception of "dog" from matching patterns in the sensory cues that we receive.

Cognitive Combat

Many challenging youth have mastered the art of using their logical systems to engage therapeutic helpers in something we identify as cognitive combat. This is an attempt by the youth to engage an adult in a war of intellect, words, or manipulative scenarios. It is when both the youth and the adult are "locked" in a battle between logical brains, based upon their experiences that have shaped their own personal logic. This use of cognitive combat can either be intentional or unintentional. The primary marker is that the logical brain is in play, where thoughts, planning and strategies are utilized in an attempt to gain power, status, or control over people or the environment. Neurologist and neuropsychiatrist Richard Restack (2006) identifies this as an attempt for two people to intentionally try to mentally outperform the other in a negative way.

When looking at cognitive combat, it is important to remember that we are a product of our experiences. Not all logic demonstrated by youth makes sense to us. In fact, we may even describe it as "illogical" from our own perspective. We have to keep in mind that we are looking at their behavior through our perspective until we have gained insight into theirs. These illogical behavioral demonstrations are frequently a youth's way of trying to say something simple such as "get away from me," "stop trying to help me; I feel worthless," or "I need something and don't know how to tell you." We must recognize the early signs of cognitive combat and refuse to engage with a youth at this level. If we do engage, the youth walks away with a more solidified experience of another adult who "fights" with him or her or who refuses to take his or her perspective. This non-therapeutic type of interaction fails to reimburse youth with new, positive experiences. To be fully in the moment with them, therapeutic helpers need to listen to their words, watch their behavior and ask them about their life stories to determine how to support them NeuroDynamically. With this experiential knowledge, we become empowered to maximize ourselves as therapeutic helpers and sculpt their experiences into constructive memories.

Story - Jamal and the "Math Gene"

Fourth period of the day was always a battle for Jamal's math teacher. To say that math was not Jamal's favorite subject was an understatement. No matter how the teacher approached it, Jamal hated math and did everything in his power to avoid it. One day, Jamal was not working on his problems during group practice time and his teacher mentioned this. Jamal responded by saying that he couldn't do it and that it ran in his family. The teacher asked for elaboration and Jamal told him that his dad was no good at math and his brother was no good at math and he was not good at math. "It's not my fault — it runs in the family." The teacher argued that the ability to do math was not genetic and that he was just making up excuses not to do his work. Jamal countered that not all the genes on the human genome had been identified and that there may, in fact, be a math gene. In his own unique way, Jamal informed the teacher that a "good teacher" would take the possibility of heredity into account and understand that not all students were genetically able to do math. The math teacher told Jamal that this was just silly and Jamal then countered that the teacher just called him stupid, so there was little wonder that he couldn't do his math. The teacher, now flustered and annoyed, continued to argue with Jamal until the bell rang. Jamal walked out of math class laughing, with no work done, leaving his math teacher frustrated and angry with himself for being manipulated by Jamal.

Jamal had engaged in an intentional round of cognitive combat with his math teacher and won. Based on prior experiences, many of our youth, like Jamal, come prepared to beat us at our own game well before we know we have even been invited to the game. They come ready and armed to fight. In adults who are not aware of how experience shapes a youth's brain, this can be a formidable challenge. However, by understanding this and employing an appropriate NDI, not engaging with them at this level, we can set the stage for new and more positive experiences that will create new pathways and ways of thinking.

The ACT QUICK Model-Positive Support
During Conflict and Crisis

Just as in the stories of Tanya and Jamal in this chapter, young people often find themselves in situations that require a therapeutic helper to either assist with logical processing for a specific moment or to help them think through a situation, being their surrogate brain. Our troubled young people have generally not had the appropriate opportunities to develop and practice the necessary reasoning and predicting skills. They do not always either make the best choices or respond in an acceptable way, creating problems for themselves and conflict or crisis with others. This provides opportunity for reimbursement of transformative experiences that will reshape and retrain the brain to become more functional and successful across numerous ecologies.

The **ACT QUICK** model involves a series of NeuroDynamic steps that consider the brain and relational needs of both the young person and the therapeutic helper. Therapeutic helpers can follow this sequence in order to respond proactively during moments of conflict and crisis. These are your moment-to-moment interactions with young people who require relational support and guidance to prevent escalation or to de-escalate if necessary. If escalation does occur, then the model provides momentary management until post-conflict/crisis supports can be put in place.

ACT QUICK is designed as an efficient tool that can be effective with a variety of issues facing youth.

The NeuroDynamic steps are as follows:

- *Assess the brain state of the child and therapeutic helper*
- *Calm the child <u>and</u> environment for safety*
- *Talk with the child using compassion and natural support*
- *Question for depth and urgency to determine level of support needed*
- *Unwrap meaning of the emotional behavior and thinking*
- *Investigate historical experience; is this new or not?*
- *Create a realistic plan, supported with strengths*
- *Keep in touch, follow-up with the youth to show ongoing support*

The table below gives a brief overview of the essential things that you need to consider for each step.

Step	Questions to Consider
Assess	What is the brain state of the child - logical (argumentative) or survival (reactive)? What is your brain state? Failure to use your thinking brain will result in cognitive combat or an amygdala war.
Calm	What brain states are in play? Who or what needs to be ecologically managed? What strategies can be implemented for the brain and body to co-regulate or self-regulate?
Talk	Is the young person calm? How can you validate emotional states and connect with the behavior? How intense are their feelings? How can you offer support?
Question	On a scale of 1 - 10 - how serious is the problem? What happened? Who was involved? How can you best assist in the resolution of the problem?
Unwrap	Find out the "why" behind the behavior. Was it done consciously or unconsciously? Move on if the answers are filled with "I don't knows"
Investigate	Is this behavior a pattern or a new behavior? Who was involved? What typically has happened if this is a recurring problem?
Create	What is a strength that a plan/strategy can be made around? Practice the strategy considering multiple scenarios. Who else needs to know about this plan?
Keep	Establish a follow-up opportunity. Stay in touch.

Novelty — The Brain Stands Up and Takes Notice

The brain loves new things. It is drawn to respond and absorb anything it sees as new. The brain actually gets excited when something novel enters the picture and catches its full attention. That is why new strategies and fresh approaches appeal to us so much. We are constantly on the lookout for a better plan or idea to help us survive well in life. Novelty kicks us out of our regular routine and into a new awareness of details.

Novelty strengthens memory. A friend calls out of the blue and the memory lingers with you long after the call is over. A tax rebate you were not expecting arrives in the mail and you talk about it with friends for days. Your memory is strengthened and your brain is refreshed. Why does this happen? When the brain experiences something novel, the hippocampus releases dopamine that speeds up the synapses or connections in the brain. There is a novelty center in the brain called the substantia nigra/ventral tegmental area. This part of the brain is also activated by unusual or unexpected experiences (either good or bad). It is linked to both the hippocampus and the amygdala and therefore exerts a major influence on learning. The memory is "locked in" and the engagement of the amygdala adds an emotional "spice" or flavor to the memory of the experience (either positive or negative). Research on novel experiences and the novelty center of the brain found that this part of the brain is not only driven by novelty, but that positive novel experiences may actually enhance learning in the context of novelty. In terms of the brain and learning, William Makepeace Thackeray was correct when he said, "Novelty has charms that our minds can hardly withstand."

Key Terms - Chapter 2

amygdala	co-regulate	neurotransmitter	self-regulation
amygdala war	dendrite	novelty	synapse
apoptosis	hemispheres	nucleus accumbens	vasopressin
axon	hippocampus	oxytocin	
cerebral cortex	metacognition	prefrontal cortex	

CHAPTER 3
Stress, Trauma, and Restoration

*Adopting the right attitude can convert a negative stress
into a positive one.*
Hans Selye

Stress

Working with challenging young people is not easy. In fact, working with typical young people can be difficult as they begin to learn how to navigate life, just because of normal developmental stressors. Stress is the number one cause of people seeking mental health assistance in the helping professions. Stress disrupts regular routines and magnifies small things into formidable challenges. People working with challenging young people need to be able to work effectively to co-manage psychological problems in others, and to do that adults must understand their own personal stressors and be able to manage them prior to working with these individuals.

An endocrinologist, Hans Selye, originally used the term stress in the 1930s to describe physiological responses in lab animals. He later broadened and popularized the term to include the perceptions and responses of humans trying to adapt to the challenges of everyday life. Used broadly, stress ranges from mild irritation to severe problems that result in a breakdown of health. In popular usage, it would include almost any event or situation between these extremes. Signs of stress can be cognitive, emotional, physical, or behavioral. Each person perceives stress differently due mainly to prior experiences and how these experiences have impacted their lives.

Some people are fragile, some are more resilient, but either way, how we react to stress is critical to our success in life.

This Is Your Brain on Stress

Our brains appraise everything that we experience. Our senses send information to the thalamus, the router of all information in the brain. It simultaneously relays the information to both the prefrontal cortex and the amygdala. This gives us two possible ways to process our experiences, the "low road" or the "high road" (LeDoux, 1996). Our brain uses the low road, from the thalamus directly to the amygdala, when our survival depends on a purely reactive, non-thinking response. The thalamus makes a quick decision. Is it good or bad, threatening or nonthreatening? Meanwhile the cortex also receives this sensory information and begins to process it. The brain compares it to other experiences in its files and this information is forwarded to the emotional brain. The emotional brain assigns an emotional tag to the experience. This message from the amygdala is then relayed to the hypothalamus and the motor regions of the brain, resulting in a physical response. This all happens in a fraction of a second and involves unconscious brain processes (Damasio, 1994).

When a threat or stressor is realized and the brain signals the body to begin preparing for flight or fight, a part of the brain called the hypothalamic-pituitary-adrenal (HPA) system is activated. The HPA system trigger the production and release of steroid hormones (glucocorticoids), including the primary stress hormone cortisol (Sapolsky, Romero & Munck, 2000). Cortisol is very important in organizing systems throughout the body (including the heart, lungs, circulation, metabolism, immune systems, and skin) to deal quickly with the impending threat (Miller, Chen, & Zhou, 2007). The HPA system also releases certain neurotransmitters (chemical messengers) called catecholamines, particularly dopamine, norepinephrine, and epinephrine (adrenaline). Catecholamines activate the amygdala, which triggers an emotional response to a stressful event (Sapolsky, 2004, Sapolsky, Romero & Munck, 2000). Adrenaline is produced and the secretion of cortisol is activated in the adrenal cortex.

Your heart rate and breathing increase, your blood pressure and blood sugar rise, and your immune response is suppressed.

During the stressful event, catecholamines also suppress activity in areas at the front of the brain concerned with short-term memory, concentration, inhibition, and rational thought. This sequence of mental events allows a person to react quickly to the threat and respond with one of the five Fs (fight, flight, freeze, feed, or fornicate – although usually it is one of the first three options). The preoccupation with the threat reduces a person's ability to make good decisions or engage in other complex cognitive process.

Stress is only intended to be a short-term solution to a threat. It gets you going and out of harm's way or it motivates you to do what needs to be done. Stress activators and modulators play significant roles in preparing the mind, and most specifically the body, for response to an overwhelming situation. They also cause inflammation in the body. Prolonged stress begins to impact vital body organs and systems in a negative way. In fact, cortisol has been linked to a variety of health problems and dysfunction, including damage to the prefrontal cortex and hippocampus.

Stress and Pressure - Good and Bad

As strange as it sounds, there is such a thing as good stress (eustress). In the short term some stress or pressure provides immediate strength that can act to motivate and inspire us. One example of this is when athletes flood their bodies with fight-or-flight adrenaline to power an explosive performance. Another example is when deadlines are used to motivate people who seem unmotivated or are having difficulty getting down to the task at hand.

However, too much stress is a bad thing (distress). For example, a demanding boss at work who creates unreasonable demands and deadlines will create distress in his or her employees. In these situations, stress responses cause our performance to suffer. In the NeuroTransactional model we use the concept of stress becoming too much for a person when pressures are greater than the available internal or external resources. This stress formula would be written as follows:

Stress = Pressures > Resources **(S=P>R)**

According to Daniel Goleman, when people are under stress, brain function moves on a continuum from the slower, logical, thought processing prefrontal cortex towards the quick moving amygdala in the midbrain – the fight or flight survival zone. The continuum can be represented by an "upside-down U with its legs spread out a bit," an idea classified by Robert Yerkes and John Dodson in 1908 (Goleman, 2006).

The Tipping Point

The Yerkes-Dodson Law explains the relationship between levels of stress (arousal) and mental performance such as learning or decision-making. Too little stress (hypostress) leads to boredom. As the level of stress increases, an individual can move upward on the "U" through levels of attention and motivation until maximum cognitive efficiency is reached. This "tipping point" differs from individual to individual.

As the challenge, or stressor, increases past this tipping point (hyperstress), it will exceed an individual's ability to handle the stress. Performance and learning begin to suffer as the amygdala function debilitates the prefrontal activity. Progressively, the brain's executive center loses control of its ability to think through situations. As the pressure intensifies, people are less able to "learn, hold information in working memory, to react flexibly and creatively, to focus attention at will, and plan and organize effectively … what neuroscientists call cognitive dysfunction" (Goleman, 2006, p.268). This is made worse when the neural circuitry from the amygdala runs to the right side of the prefrontal cortex, causing people to fixate on the cause of the stress. This fixation undermines the capacity for additional learning and makes the generation of new ideas impossible. Essentially, it "hijacks" attention. In addition, anxiety or stress causes the brain to secrete high levels of the stress hormone cortisol and the neuroreceptor norepinephrine. This causes further interference with the processes for learning and memory.

Learning and memory are impacted because the hippocampus is damaged by prolonged exposure to cortisol. This exposure both reduces the existing number of neurons and slows the rate at which new neurons are added. In effect, it shrinks the overall volume of the hippocampus. However, the good news is that this is not a permanent state. Once the stress or trauma is dealt with, the hippocampus regains neurons and returns to its original size (Elizinga & Roelofs, 2005). While cortisol impairs the hippocampus, it stimulates the amygdala. This causes us to focus on how we feel instead of what is actually going on, and it is this emotional response that we will remember (Goleman, 2006).

Balance is critical. We need a little stress in life. If we are lacking the necessary levels of pressure to do certain things we will suffer. However, persistent stress that is not resolved through coping or adaptation is not good for us either. The difference between which experiences will cause eustress or distress is determined by the disparity of a person's resources to cope and his or her personal expectations.

Stress, Abuse, and Trauma

In relational work, there are three commonly accepted levels of stress. First, the general stress state, or acute stress, that occurs and is typical in day-to-day events that one is faced with. The second is abuse or conflict that is a more significant form of stress (chronic stress). This form of stress is intense and can cause us to reevaluate our circumstances. Finally there is trauma. The DSM IV (American Psychiatric Association, 2000) defines trauma as "a direct personal experience of an event that involves actual or threatened death or serious injury, or other threat to one's physical integrity; or witnessing an event that involves death, injury, or a threat to the physical integrity of another person; or learning about unexpected or violent death, serious harm, or threat of death or injury experienced by a family member or other close associate. The person's response to the event must involve fear, helplessness, or horror (or in children, the response must involve disorganized or agitated behavior)."

As a general rule, chronic abuse and trauma impede brain maturation and interfere with the normal hierarchical development and integration of the brain systems. Keep in mind that the brain is molded by experience. Every sight, sound, and thought leaves an imprint on specific neural circuits, modifying the way future sights, sounds, and thoughts will be perceived. All relationships, and especially primary relationships, impact the developing brain profoundly, for better or worse. When children feel safe and supported, their brains develop in a very coherent manner; but if they don't feel safe and connected in their primary relationships, their brains develop in a disrupted way.

Trauma Informed Care

Over the last 20 years there has been increasing recognition of the role that trauma plays in a wide range of problems that our young people experience. The growing knowledge base about how trauma affects people is now being used to inform changes in how we think and what we do. By definition, trauma-informed practice is policy and practice based on what we know from research about trauma and how it affects people. This trauma-informed NeuroTransactional model considers the connections between traumatic events and the neurobiological and behavioral implications.

Strength through Stress

Successful adaptation and survival in life is frequently associated with the ability to see stressful and challenging situations as opportunities for growth instead of potentially negative or threatening. Gregg Jacobs (2003) of Harvard Medical School states that, "stress hardy individuals have a sense of control over events in their lives, a strong commitment to something outside of themselves" and "take better advantage of social support" (pp.113–114). Studies in stress hardiness have shown that when one has a sense of control, even if it is not realistic, the potential for positive outcomes is greatly increased. This sense of control leads to a more fulfilling life characterized by feelings of contentment and happiness.

Youth who have experienced significant adversity in life, and who do not display this type of positive coping system, will inevitably need therapeutic helpers to "be with" them in moments of challenge and cognitively guide them through tough scenarios. In these instances, the primary goal of the therapeutic helper is to assist the youth in restructuring their inappropriate thinking patterns so that hope is infused into even the most difficult of circumstances. When the therapeutic helper and the youth have experienced sufficient opportunities to face challenges together successfully, the therapeutic helper should begin to withdraw the direct support and allow the youth to maximize his or her new resources more independently. Most youth who display poor coping strategies have not been mentored by hopeful, competent adults. These youth will need many opportunities to retrain the brain that "things can be better."

The Many Faces of Trauma

Trauma can have many different faces. Trauma can be a single overwhelming event or it can be complex - repeated victimizations either later in life or beginning in early childhood. It can be impersonal - natural disasters, fire, or war. It can be interpersonal - the deliberate threat or injury in the context of an interpersonal interaction (stranger rape, criminal assault, sexual harassment, combat). It can be relational - the deliberate threat or injury in the context of a relationship where the victim has some level of emotional involvement. Or it can be developmental - inflicted on infants and children unconsciously and most often without malicious intent by adult caregivers who are unaware of children's social and emotional needs (Stien & Kendall, 2004).

Infants and children require energetic attunement, skin-to-skin and eye-to-eye contact, kind and comforting words, protection and safety from their mother during pregnancy, birth, and the first years of life. Unfortunately, some parents have not been educated about children's social and emotional needs and lack skills for supporting their child emotionally when they become upset. They also may have never fully experienced emotional attunement with their own parents when they were children. This makes it difficult for them to respond to their children's needs for nurturing, protection, safety and guidance in timely and appropriate ways. These parents also do not connect the deficiencies in their experiences with their parents with their own day-to-day struggles to effectively parent their own children.

Regardless of the type of trauma, trauma is an experience. Ultimately it is the human brain that processes and internalizes traumatic experiences. Understanding the organization, function, and development of the human brain and brain-mediated responses to threat are the keys to understanding traumatized young people.

According to Bruce Perry, a senior fellow of the Child Trauma Academy in Houston, neurons form and most migrate to their final location and then begin to differentiate in utero. Others complete their journey after birth. But all continue to differentiate until they are ready to perform their specific functions. The brain organizes and develops from the bottom up. As the brain develops from bottom to top, this process is influenced by a host of chemical signals (neurotransmitters, hormones and modulators). These signals help target cells to move, differentiate, and form synaptic connections. These crucial neural networks originate in the lower brain areas and spread up to all other parts of the developing brain (Perry, Pollard, Blakely, Baker, & Vigilante, 1995). These systems are then able to communicate across multiple regions of the brain simultaneously. This guides development later in life. Impairment in the organization and functioning of these systems can result in a cascade of dysfunction from the lower regions up to all the target areas higher in the brain (Perry, 2009). Impairments during pregnancy, like maternal stress, drugs and alcohol, malnutrition, neglect, or abuse in early childhood, can all disrupt normal development.

The organization of higher parts of the brain depends upon information from the lower parts of the brain. Regulated, synchronous neural information from the lower regions of the brain allows the higher areas of the brain to organize in healthy ways. When the neural activity from the lower areas of the brain is dysregulated, asynchronous, and extreme, the higher areas will organize in an unhealthy or abnormal way (Perry, 2009).

Why Trauma Impacts Some People More Than Others

Everyone reacts differently to trauma. Experiences and perceptions of a traumatic event can vary depending on the developmental stage or age of the young person. Young people who have a history of behavioral or emotional difficulties, familial stresses, academic concerns, or prior exposure to trauma are more likely to find a traumatic event profoundly significant. The perceived level of severity of the event also impacts the effect of the trauma; the greater the perception of a threat to life, injury to self, family impact, property damage, or personal loss, the more profound the traumatic impact (Cohen, Deblinger, Mannarino, & de Arellano, 2001; Roer-Strier, 2001).

Individual reactions are also dependent on how parents and other adults express their reactions after a traumatic event. In many post-trauma or post-disaster situations, basic needs like housing and food can be compromised. A lack of predictability due to moving, change of schools, and compromised living conditions can cause additional distress and can make adjustment and recovery more difficult. The same factors that can affect young people can also impact parents and family members. If the event is causing family members to feel more anxious and/or fearful, they can exhibit overprotective behaviors or maladaptive coping responses potentially making the young person more fearful and less able to cope (NCTSN, 2012). Increased traumatization can also occur from either listening to others discuss the event at length or attending to media focus. Constant reminder of loss and threat can cause a wide fluctuation in behavioral and emotional reactions and an awareness of the impact on the family and how they are responding to it is important.

Experience Becomes Biology

Childhood relational trauma, trauma at the hands of those closest to young people, is viewed as being the most difficult to treat and has the most impact on the brain. Trauma between people is powerful and creates experiences that are imprinted on the brain for a lifetime. Details of the trauma may surface over a lifespan if left without proper support. The sensory system is very sensitive to bits and pieces of the world that may alert youth to the potential of a similar threat or experience like the one in the past. Traumatic experiences can leave the brain in a hyper-alert state and result in over-reactions to typical circumstances or the person disconnecting with the experiences in order to make them go away. In either case, the memories exist and will impact the youth in life.

How Trauma Affects the Body and Behavior - Polyvagal Theory

Most of us are familiar with the fight or flight response - the sympathetic nervous system's response to a threatening stimulus. It is a response that helps us survive and depending on the threat and our personal assessment of our ability to cope with it - we either fight, flee, freeze and our body responds by producing hormones, slowing digestion, constricting blood vessels, and increasing the heart rate. When the threat or stress is removed, the parasympathetic system returns the body to its normal state, reversing these physiological reactions - "rest and digest". For years, it was believed that these systems worked in a reciprocal fashion, but in 1994, behavioral neuroscientist Stephen Porges discovered a third nervous system response that he called the social engagement system (SES). The SES response is activated when we feel safe in our surroundings, allows us to connect with others, and encourages the parasympathetic system to produce chemicals that help us feel content and at peace (Porges et al., 1994).

Porges believed that all three systems worked together and identified three branches of the vagal nerve that activated physiological responses through the sympathetic and parasympathetic systems. The ventral branch assists the sympathetic nervous system when the system is not threatened allowing the body to create a balance between stimulation and relaxation.

Another branch of the nerve (dorsal) assists the sympathetic system when it becomes overloaded in a threatening situation by instigating the freeze response. He noted that this shutdown response also occurs when a person is feeling shame or rejection.

Unresolved trauma puts people in a perpetual state of hypervigilance or fight or flight and this constant feeling of not being safe can overload the sympathetic system and result in a shutdown response, restricting the positive aspects of the social engagement system. When our social engagement systems are not functioning properly, we have difficulty accurately perceiving vocal tones and facial expressions (Porges, 2009) and we may appear to over-react to what most would consider a neutral stimulus. In order to work effectively with trauma affected individuals, they need to feel safe enough to move from that dorsal response to a calmer and more regulated ventral state. Many techniques can be used to move to the calmer ventral state but one of the simplest was identified by Porges when he noted that extending exhalations and shorter inhalations for a period of time, activated the calming parasympathetic system (Porges, 2011). Exactly how this happens is not fully understood but slow regular breathing seems to play a major role in well-attuned communication and connection with others (Miller et al., 2017).

Effects of Relational Trauma

One of the most significant forms of trauma occurs at the relational level. Abuse and extreme stress during childhood can impair early brain development and metabolic and immune system function, leading to chronic health problems, especially when the stress is inflicted by those in close relationship with the young person. This happens in part because child abuse leaves epigenetic marks on a child's genes that can alter fundamental biological processes increasing their risk for a wide range of physical and psychiatric health conditions. These genetic markers also make them more susceptible to developing post-traumatic stress disorder if they experience other types of trauma later in life. Experience becomes biology.

According to Schore, (2000) the most profound effect of early ongoing childhood trauma is the limited development of the right hemisphere of the brain. Normally, the right hemisphere processes social and emotional information. The right frontal cortex modulates emotions and responds to social cues such as facial expressions. At the same time, aggression is modulated through a right hemisphere self-regulating system that operates on an unconscious level. These systems can develop only in a secure, nurturing environment.

Schore believes that through "affect synchrony," a child first experiences communication by learning to modify his or her behavior in response to signals put out by the caregiver and the caregiver's response to signals expressed by the child. When an infant is stressed or over-aroused, the caregiver responds in a reparative way that allows the child to develop internal self-soothing mechanisms and over time learn how to repair or regulate his or her emotional state. Children who can do this are more resilient under stress.

Neglected or abused children experience unusually high levels of arousal and no opportunity for interactive repair. Early trauma not only leads to impaired development, it deprives the child of normal developmental experiences (Schore, 2003). By the time these children enter adolescence and adulthood, they exhibit hostile, aggressive personalities, struggle with conventional social cues, and have difficulty reading others' facial expressions. They also appear unconcerned about how their behavior affects others. Under threat or stress, they will often respond in an aggressive manner.

Lack of cooperation between hemispheres can also create other symptoms. Generally negative emotions such as fear are processed in the right hemisphere and positive emotions such as affection and happiness are processed in the left. If the hemispheres are not operating together, these emotions cannot be experienced at the same time.

Maltreated children often divide people into categories of "all good" and "all bad" rather than developing a more balanced view of others.

Lack of integration between hemispheres may contribute to dissociative ego states, and symptoms such as trance states and depersonalization. When activity in the left hemisphere is diminished, perceptions may seem timeless and disconnected because the emotions that are generated in the right hemisphere cannot be transformed into words, placed in context, or assigned meaning (Stien & Kendall, 2004).

Stress, Trauma, and Memory

Chronic stress and trauma can also damage the youth's hippocampus, affecting memory storage and retrieval. Under normal developmental circumstances, memory allows us to register the world outside us. A person breaks down an experience into components (location, time of day, emotional feel, and physical characteristics) and files them away in separate areas of the brain. Normally the conscious and unconscious memory systems work together. The conscious system, mediated by the hippocampus, contains experiences that we can readily retrieve and talk about. The amygdala, one of the brain systems in charge of the unconscious, establishes the value of an experience or emotional memory.

The amygdala is reasonably developed at birth. The hippocampus isn't fully mature until age three or four. Both systems are independent and interdependent, as most stimuli activate both. Think back to the scenario described in Chapter 1 where you narrowly avoided being hit by a motorcycle. You jumped back before you were even aware of exactly what had happened. Your heart was pounding and your hands were shaking as you realized what could have just happened. For the next little while, every time you hear the sound of a motorcycle close by it will trigger an unconscious memory and your amygdala will activate a body response. Your hippocampus, directing your conscious memory, will make you remember the near miss. Eventually the two types of memories become fused and potentially can become a long-term memory. The brain structures working together allow for the development of conscious emotional memories. We will remember the experience in total, but after it is stored in long-term memory we remember the incident without the full-blown emotional reaction.

Most researchers believe that memory processes fail because high levels of stress-related chemicals impair the functioning of critical brain structures, especially the hippocampus (Elzinga & Roelofs, 2005). When the hippocampus cannot properly encode memories (integrate sensory, motor, visual, and auditory) the memory can only be retrieved in fragments, so that the individual is unable to put the whole story together (Brown, Chen, Johnson, Salzinger, 1998). Extreme stress is also related to a breakdown in the functioning of not only the hippocampus, but also parts of the prefrontal cortex. These parts normally modulate and inhibit the amygdala's response to fearful stimuli. However, in trauma victims this doesn't happen so they can't distinguish the real thing from a similar but not threatening event. They end up with abnormal re-experiencing of traumatic memories and a long duration of fearful responses.

Trauma and Abuse Re-experienced

Although traumatized adults are typically challenged by intrusive thoughts and images, children tend to re-experience trauma differently. They will often have nightmares, re-enact the events in art or play, re-enact the event behaviorally, or express it through body memories (Perry, 2006, Stien & Kendall, 2004).

Flashbacks often take the form of terrifying dreams, replaying the disturbing event with all the accompanying feelings of terror and despair. Normally children's bad dreams reflect normal developmental fears and hopes. After trauma, dreams often become very literal and repetitive. Normally, they would wake up before being caught in a bad dream about being chased by an animal. In post-trauma dreams, they may end up being attacked or even killed.

Children also re-experience trauma through play that re-enacts elements or themes of the event. Normal play is three-dimensional. It is creative and helps them problem solve. Traumatic play is two-dimensional or monotonous, and leads to stagnation rather than growth. The same theme keeps resurfacing: helplessness, unpredictability, terror, and death.

Behavioral re-enactments resemble traumatic play closely although the child experiences each activity differently. It involves patterns of everyday behavior that incorporate aspects of the trauma. For example, sexually provocative behavior can be a way of re-enacting sexual abuse, even though the youngster might explain the behavior as "just me."

Body memories are a form of physical discomfort. Under stress a child may experience the same uncomfortable sensations associated with the trauma. Alternately, he or she can experience psychosomatic symptoms such as persistent headaches and migraines, abdominal tract problems, a racing heart, light-headedness, and dizziness.

Signs and Symptoms of Trauma and Abuse

In addition to the four ways of experiencing trauma, children can manifest some or all of the following symptoms: physical symptoms with no organic cause; feelings of anxiety; avoidance of situations that remind them of their trauma; heightened arousal (poor concentration, sleep problems, depression, or sadness); or externalized symptoms, such as irritability or temper tantrums. They can also develop an exaggerated startle response.

You can also see an oscillation between extreme arousal and numbed responsiveness. These children often engage in self-destructive behavior to help regulate emotional states. They do this because self-harm or provoking interpersonal conflict triggers the brain's natural calming mechanisms. They show signs of cognitive impairment, a rigid style of thinking, and difficulties with assimilation and accommodation. Their thinking processes lag behind their peers and this can contribute to learning problems. They will have a great deal of difficulty relating to others. They avoid eye contact, are hyper-vigilant, and withdraw.

Hyperactivity and oppositional behavior are not uncommon. They have an obsessive need to be in control that makes it hard for those who work with them. They become hopeless about the future and express this as despair or hate and revenge.

The potential social implications of trauma and abuse cannot be ignored. Exposure to neglect and abuse may result in reduced ability to seek rewarding relationships and a reduced commitment to societal and cultural values. Artificial and quick rewards become attractive. Unmet bonding needs increase allure to gangs, sects, and cults with violent and authoritarian values, which can create safety issues for these young people.

Story - "Swearing at You Means I Like You"

Mary was 17 when her teacher first met her. Prior teacher reports indicated that she was oppositional, rude, and not interested in her schoolwork. She was overly vigilant and very on edge. While evidently a very bright young lady, her work and attitude had been deteriorating since the school year started. She had also begun to cut herself. Her mother had refused referral to any clinical services. By January, her behavior and performance at school had deteriorated to the point where she was suspended and referred to an off-campus alternative program. She arrived covered in scars and open cuts (arms, legs, and stomach) and an "I hate the world and you in particular" attitude.

Initially, she would not talk to her teacher at all. She sat down, crossed her legs and arms, and stared at the teacher for days while the teacher and Mary had a rather one-sided conversation (if that's possible). If the teacher asked her to do anything academic, she would do it and then throw it at her or slam it on her desk, but refused to participate in the daily group sessions. Once she decided to talk, she was verbally and emotionally abusive and tried very hard to get the teacher to suspend her or give up on her. The teacher did her best to ignore the abuse and focus on the positive. Her academics were outstanding when she chose to do her work. She attended regularly and the teacher noticed over time that the cutting had stopped and most physical wounds were healing. One day she looked up from her work and told the other students and the teacher that they were a bunch of "idiots" (in slightly more descriptive terminology with several choice expletives) and the teacher smiled and commented to no one in particular that it seemed that Mary did not like the teacher or the group very much. Mary looked quite surprised and said, "Of course I like you — swearing at you is how I show it. If I didn't like you, I wouldn't waste my breath on you at all." This provided an opportunity to begin a conversation and as she started to open up, bits and pieces of her life were slowly shared.

Mary had been severely neglected as a child. She was an infringement on her mother's social life and was left at home with the younger siblings, serving as the in-house childcare provider while her mother partied and went to the bar. Mom found a live-in boyfriend and had moved him into a basement suite, joining him there and leaving Mary and her three younger brothers and sisters to fend for themselves upstairs. Mary had been holding things together fairly well until the new boyfriend started verbally abusing her, telling her that she was useless and ugly and would never find a boyfriend. Mom was aware of what was happening but blamed Mary. It was around that time that she started to cut herself and create problems at school.

Initially, Mary needed to find someone who was supportive and that she could learn to trust. It was important for her to feel safe, but it was also helpful for her to have someone who would listen. While they had a long way to go, Mary and her teacher had made the first steps towards a more transformative relationship, providing her with positive and affirming experiences with another person.

Culture and Trauma

In addition to the factors just discussed, culture influences our perception of what type of threat is perceived as traumatic and how we interpret the meaning of the traumatic event. Culture also influences how individuals and communities experience and express traumatic distress, disclose their experiences, and seek support and help. Historical and/or multigenerational trauma (cumulative emotional and psychological wounding over the lifespan and across generations, emanating from massive group trauma (Yellow Horse Brave Heart, 1999) can affect the overall perception that a group has towards the world in general and the likelihood of the effectiveness of existing social institutions to provide support and care. Understanding the experiences of communities affected by historical or multigenerational trauma is important to begin the healing process. On a positive note, cultures may also help define healthy pathways to new lives after trauma. The routines and traditions of particular cultures can help trauma survivors regain a feeling of predictability and control in their lives and help them heal.

Working with Trauma Impacted Young People

Caring for or working with young people who have been affected by trauma can be stressful and can trigger personal reactions (Figley, 1995). Our focus is often on the young person, helping them to manage their behavioral and emotional reactions, and it is easy to forget that our emotions can also be impacted. Often we end up feeling overwhelmed, exhausted, and frustrated by the reactions of the young person and experience "empathy fatigue" - a form of secondary traumatic stress disorder. It is vitally important that anyone working with traumatized young people monitor their personal reactions, emotions, and needs and seek support. This is particularly important if the adults were involved in the trauma as unresolved traumatic issues can easily rise to the surface. Proper self-care improves both the quality of care for the young people and your personal professional capacity.

Hope and Opportunity through Neuroplasticity

All interpersonal interactions affect the brain. We know that how our brain's function determines how we perceive, think, and behave and our emotions also affect these things. Secure, non-threatening environments for all people will help us function at maximum cognitive efficiency. In abused children, positive therapeutic relationships can interactively regulate negative states and thus help buffer the effects of traumatic stress. To help children affected by trauma and stress, we must help to create an environment that enhances positive brain development and a safe environment to experience new relationships. New and better experiences can change their brains. It is never too late. We always have a window of hope and opportunity due to the plasticity of the brain

Key Terms - Chapter 3

adrenaline	Hyperstress
cortisol	Hypostress
distress	Stress
eustress	stress formula
executive center	trauma

CHAPTER 4
Social Connectedness

When you listen with empathy to another person, you give
that person psychological air.
Steven Covey

Empathic Connections

Being social is simply not enough to thrive in the human realm. We can be social and not friendly or welcoming. However, when we connect positively with others, be that momentarily or over an extended period, we learn various aspects of their individual nuances. We attune to some or all of these social cues and reminders. Attunement involves recognizing aspects that are either good or bad in others, in ourselves, and between one another. Attunement also means being "in synch" with others so that we can better connect and survive.

One way we attune with others is through empathy. We have the capacity to infer what others are thinking or feeling (mindfulness) allowing us to recognize that our views may not be the same as others but we can also share feelings or empathize with each other. Empathy is conjointly resonating with what others feel - the joy, the sadness or the pain. Despite the fact that we resonate with what they feel, we generally realize that the emotion we are experiencing is theirs and is not our own personal feeling. Sharing positive emotions is pleasant but sharing negative emotions can cause suffering. If the line between self and other blurs, that suffering can become distress (Singer & Klimecki, 2014).

In order to avoid the negative implications of shared distress that is often experienced in helping professions, Singer suggests responding with compassion. Instead of sharing the negative feelings and emotions, compassion allows us to feel warmth and concern for others and a desire to help them feel better. Compassion is "feeling for and not feeling with the other (Singer & Klimecki, 2014, p. 875). By being able to respond compassionately, we act on our empathy in a positive way that allows us to feel good about what we are doing rather than being dragged down by the enormity of the situation. We feel motivated to work for positive change. In chapter 1 we said that dopamine not only has the power to create the motivation for us to try something new, it also provides us with a new sense of hope. Compassionate response is a dopamine producing response and we need dopamine to avoid empathy fatigue and burnout.

Many young people that we work with suffer from a restricted ability to attune that causes them to misread or misinterpret the intentions of others. This may mean that they perceive the world as either an overly safe or unusually threatening place to be. They lack the necessary interpretive social balance to navigate the world effectively. Without balance, there will be disruption.

Social strength requires us to think empathetically and compassionately so that we not only are able to access and feel our own emotions, but that we are also able to put our personal needs aside and imagine the feelings of others. We must be able to respond to visual cues and body language of others. This means that we have conscious control over our ability to focus, shift attention, and self-regulate under stress. Biologically, the parts of the brain that are associated with high levels of emotional regulation, impulse control, and empathic response develop and take shape in positive relational environments in infancy. Early nurturance plays a vital role in the development and integration of diverse systems within our brains. Optimal sculpting of the thinking part of the brain through healthy early relationships allows us to think well of ourselves, trust others, regulate our emotions, maintain positive expectations, and utilize our intellectual and emotional intelligence in moment-to-moment problem solving.

University of Chicago psychologist Milhaly Csikszentmihalyi calls this "flow." It is the fluid and synchronized movement of information throughout the brain and body. According to Csikszentmihalyi (1990), when information moves from one area of the brain to another, we process experience through all modalities of sensory perception: images, thoughts, behavior, and sensations. However, when this integration has not developed normally, when experiences have not allowed the integration of all the systems of the brain, young people get "stuck" in one state or area of the brain, often in a fear response. Young people operating from a fear response often lack empathic capacities and cannot put themselves in another's place.

In order to move from the spot where they are stuck, these youths need to experience a sense of emotional attunement with a significant adult in their lives. Their brains need to connect with another human brain and they need to be able to move from the dorsal vagal response to the ventral vagal response. Daniel Siegel calls this "feeling felt." When two brains work together, the activation of changes in the brain opens up the possibility for transformation to greater levels of well-being. This includes the ability to see and understand how others feel while still maintaining a personal sense of self. Being able to attune interpersonally is the first step towards true empathy. If an attuned, secure relationship can be maintained over time, people can become less fearful and more able to share in the experiences of others and develop more integrated circuits across the systems of the brain.

Story – Byron: Starting to "Feel" ... Better than Before

Byron had spent a great deal of time in and out of anger management classes. His teachers complained that he was "stuck in a rut" and was not able to move forward. He seemed to understand what he was taught in his sessions intellectually, but was not able to transfer those skills into his interactions in the "real world." He consistently blamed others for his problems and could not seem to make a connection between his behavior and the reactions that others had to him. The off-campus teacher who was working with him received a call from the referring school telling him that some money had disappeared from a teacher's purse and that they suspected Byron had taken it. The teacher working with him was asked to talk to him about this. To his surprise, Byron admitted it immediately, and did so with a smile on his face. He felt that she "deserved" to have it taken. Anyone who was stupid enough to leave her purse where others could access it deserved to lose her valuables. He commented, with a very straight face, that this was a high school and not in the best part of town, what the heck did she expect? No matter how hard the teacher tried to get him to see another side of the story, he was unable to get Byron to understand that he had caused another person to be in pain. In his mind, the victim had this "coming to her" and if he had been that dumb and lost his valuables to some opportunistic thief he would have deserved it too. Byron was unable to see beyond his immediate needs and wants and certainly unable to feel how another person felt. He was disconnected to the feelings of others, which was allowing him to do and say things that hurt people around him. Byron lacked the insight to connect positively and simply needed more evidence that it was better to connect in "good" ways, rather than "negative" ways. He was good at the negative connections, but the good connections were foreign territory to Byron. He needed more proof.

The teacher had many discussions like this one over the months they worked together. Each time, he tried to get Byron to see the other person's perspective. It got to the point where Byron would mock the teacher as he brought it up, calling him a "goody two-shoes do-gooder." The teacher kept smiling and persevering. While Byron was not verbalizing the things that the teacher initially hoped to hear, he noticed that Byron had begun to use him as a "surrogate brain." When he got into trouble at school, which happened fairly regularly, he would immediately bolt over to the teacher's office and try to justify his behavior. When the teacher reframed his behavior and started to instill empathic awareness of how what he was doing was impacting others, he would frequently argue on his own behalf that he was "wiser and trickier than the rest." The teacher remained dedicated to instilling empathy into the conversations, redirecting the self-centered approach he was taking to a more interpersonal approach. He constantly encouraged Byron to put himself in the hypothetical "shoes" of the other persons – a place he did not frequently visit. Although on most occasions he would attempt to engage the teacher in arguments and debates, he eventually accepted some of the teacher's ideas and suggestions, albeit they were not always demonstrated in exactly the ways the teacher had hoped for.

One morning several months after the money incident, another student in a group session he was involved in was not having a good day and was verbally abusive to the teacher. Byron immediately intervened and said something surprising. He told the other student to "shut up" because she was "making (the teacher) feel bad." Byron could be overpowering, both verbally and physically, but he never stood up for others, especially teachers. Byron's behavior stopped everyone in their tracks. This was something new.

Although his choice of words was not ideal, his actions were starting to shift from himself to others. Now there was a small sign of empathy beginning to emerge. After the group was done, the teacher pulled Byron aside and asked him about his actions. He mumbled something like "whatever" and started to walk away. The teacher asked Byron why he spoke up when the other student was cursing and screaming. Byron said it was stupid for the other student to be yelling and screaming at someone as it only "pisses people off" and makes them not "want to be around you" plus it was "rude." It was in this brief moment of clarity that the teacher knew he had made a connection with Byron, one possibly strong enough to generalize to others. If he could connect with Byron, he could connect Byron with others. The teacher was now in possession of a powerful relationship that could transform a disconnected Byron. He was now being relationally retrained to connect better with people around him.

Why We Need Positive Relationships

Relationships are where we find our "natural habitat." Without mutually stimulating interactions, people and neurons wither and die. For human babies, survival doesn't depend on how fast they can run or how well they can hunt, but rather on the ability of their caretakers to detect the needs and intentions of those around them. For humans, other people are our primary environment (Cozolino, 2006).

If we are successful in relationships, we will have our physiological and emotional needs met. Survival of the fittest for humans is entirely dependent upon our ability to adapt to our ecology and environment. Good relationships and experiences are instrumental in the growth and development of the many systems within our brains and help us to survive well. "Optimal sculpting and development of the brain through healthy early relationships allows us to: think well of ourselves, trust others, regulate our emotions, maintain positive expectations, and utilize our intellectual and emotional intelligence in moment-to-moment problem solving" (Cozolino, 2006, p.14).

Many youths with turbulent histories have dysregulated brain systems that are not yet equipped to manage the world around them. Therapeutic helpers must be able to help young people raise their levels of competence by modeling and providing "in the moment support" or proactive practice sessions. When youth see the trained adult is competent and capable, their brains allow them to connect more deeply and the relationship is fortified and ripe for more intensive growth. We need positive relationships because, according to Cozolino, "those who are nurtured best survive best."

Mirror Neurons – Monkey See Monkey Do

A new type of neuron discovered in the early 1990s called a mirror neuron could help explain how we learn through mimicry and why we empathize with others. Mirror neurons are a type of brain cell that respond equally when we perform an action and when we witness someone else perform the same action. They were first discovered in the early 1990s, when a team of Italian researchers found individual neurons in the brains of macaque monkeys that fired both when the monkeys grabbed an object and also when the monkeys watched another primate grab the same object.

These neurons are specifically in charge of imitating others. Within our brain, we are constantly mimicking the behavioral presentations of others in an effort to learn more about the people with whom we interact. This constant evaluation allows us to read and understand a variety of people and their intentions. We build an internal "resource manual" that we consistently call upon without even knowing it. This internal manual enables us to predict the intentions of others by comparing their actions with the actions of others in our past. Mirror neurons lie at the crossroads of the processing of inner and outer experience, where multiple networks of visual, motor, and emotional processing converge (Cozolino, 2006, Iacoboni et al., 2001). Observing the attainment of a goal motivates and reinforces the learning of the sequence of behavior necessary for obtaining it. Mirror neurons link observation and motor programs, so observing becomes a way to rehearse.

We still have a great deal to learn about mirror neurons. Researchers in the field believe that mirror neurons allow us to react to others, move with others, and speculate about what others are potentially thinking. They link neural networks within our own brains and link us to each other. It seems that they are a very important part of our social brains.

Mirror neurons also allow us to read and understand the social meaning of others' behavior and their emotional state (Iacoboni, 2008). This ability to identify with and understand another's situation, feelings, and motives allows us to have empathy for others. Like all abilities, the empathic attunement that mirror neurons provide us can be used in positive or negative ways. Understanding others' emotional states can be helpful in our everyday interactions and relationships. They allow us to respond appropriately in social situations. Not all forms of empathy are positive, as attunement to others opens the door for some to use empathic awareness to manipulate people by identifying and exploiting their vulnerabilities and weaknesses. So, empathic attunement by itself is not sufficient to bring forth "goodness" in people. Empathy is a prerequisite to understanding others so that we might care for them. Experience provides the opportunity for emotional attunement. Internal motivation then helps us to "want to care." When this occurs, we then have the ability to act compassionately.

Eye Gaze

Eye gaze also plays a central role in social communication. It provides information, regulates interactions, expresses intimacy or threat, exercises social control, and facilitates coordination and cooperation. When we follow another's gaze focused elsewhere, we turn our attention to a shared processing of the external environment. Brains are analyzing both the direction and object of the gaze.

As another person's gaze shifts to us, brain activation increases in the amygdala, as well as the insula, cingulate, frontal, and temporal cortices. This analysis is very rapid, as it is significant for physical safety and reproductive success. You can actually feel the shift as someone makes eye contact. Your brain goes on alert.

While eye gaze is important, the pupil size is also a way we can determine our relative safety. Without knowing it, we study the size of people's pupils constantly. Pupil size is very important. The amygdala is very sensitive to a change in the pupil size of others. Eye widening can be a signal of heightened vigilance and arousal on the part of the expresser, indicating that this individual has noticed something that requires attention in the immediate environment. The human amygdala is sensitive to signals such as these in part because of the outcomes of these expressions in the past allowing us to predict our safety and survival in the present.

What's in a Face?

Facial expressions (particularly emotionally expressive ones like disgust, fear, joy, surprise, sadness, and anger) are the primary transmitters of social bonding and survival information. As it is to eye gaze and pupil size, the amygdala is also responsive to facial expressions. From birth, our interactions with others help us to learn how best to read the faces of those around us and successfully navigate our environment. Most of the detection, processing, interpreting, and reacting to facial expressions that we do on a day-to-day basis, happens unconsciously. It can become conscious in situations where we are more invested in the situation at hand, such as in an emotional discussion with a loved one or in a situation where we feel threatened.

Reading facial expressions requires the coordination of many brain systems. Core systems for visual analysis help us with the changeable aspects of facial expressions and eye gaze. Extended systems help us to contextualize visual information, like predicting actions; to determine emotional meaning; to identify, name and add autobiographical information; and to apply internal models of behavior to our interpretations. Even the type of expression can activate multiple systems in the brain. Faces judged as fearful or untrustworthy will activate the amygdala in both hemispheres as well as the right insula cortex. The insula helps us put the fear reaction in personal, interpersonal, and space-time context. If a person looks afraid of us, it is the insula that would allow us to see the look of fear, but realize that we could feel safe. Faces that are judged as having a positive emotion (happiness or joy) activate the prefrontal cortex, the right anterior cingulate, and the amygdala in the left hemisphere. Interestingly, there has been less study of positive expressions because happiness has not been perceived as very important from an evolutionary perspective. Enjoying yourself while surviving apparently was not a priority. It is also important to keep in mind that while faces provide a great deal of data for the brain, we don't just read facial expressions. Appraisal for survival also considers posture, orientation, proximity, and movement. The ability to read body language accurately is also important to surviving and surviving well.

Key Terms - Chapter 4

appraisal	facial expressions
dysregulation (brain)	mirror neurons
eye gaze	

CHAPTER 5
NeuroDynamic Support and Reimbursement

Unless someone like you cares a whole awful lot, nothing is
going to get better. It's not.
Dr. Seuss

What You See Is Not Always What You Get

Dealing with young people's difficult behavior is often one of the most challenging things that therapeutic helpers have to do. When confronted with actions that are physically or verbally abusive, it is very hard not to take it personally and get pulled into the fray. We know that engaging negatively with the challenging behavior and becoming counter-aggressive is NeuroDynamically ineffective, relationally damaging, and can escalate to intolerable or even dangerous levels. However, challenging behavior is very much like an iceberg. You only see a part of it and what you do see does not come close to giving you a clear picture of what you are encountering.

It might be helpful to think of challenging behavior as a symptom rather than the cause. It is a form of communication, albeit usually a rather unpleasant one for the person on the receiving end of it. Difficult behavior often occurs when young people either don't know exactly what is bothering them, or when words just can't define how they perceive their situation.

They can feel overwhelmed, threatened, and unable to communicate their wants and needs effectively.

It is important that we never presume to understand the reasons for the behavior. Whatever your assumption is it is only a guess and may often be a relatively uninformed one from a NeuroTransactional perspective. Even if you have worked with a young person for an extended period of time, if you make assumptions without deeper investigation, you are setting yourself up for potential failure. As Lemony Snicket said in *The Austere Academy*, "Assumptions are dangerous things to make, and like all dangerous things . . . .if you make even the tiniest mistake you can find yourself in terrible trouble".

Essential Questions to Consider

To avoid finding yourself in terrible trouble, ask yourself these kinds of questions:

- Is this behavior new or have I seen this before? If new, what was the antecedent? If you have seen it before, is the situation in which it is occurring similar or different and how so?
- When does this behavior happen? Is it place/person dependent? What is happening at this time?
- What happened before, after, or during the behavior? Is there something going on that I am totally unaware of even if I think I saw everything that happened?
- What time does this behavior happen?
- Who or what is involved or affected? Is it time dependent? Is there an unmet need that triggers it at this particular time?

Realistically, most people do not want to misbehave, act out, or meltdown. Nor do they want the negative feedback and ensuing personal stress that come with these incidents. You must look beyond the behavior to discover the cause of the resistance. Consider the following:

Story – Jacob and the "Assumption"

A young person in a residential setting was exhibiting a particularly upsetting behavior – he was fecal smearing. Needless to say this was very upsetting to those working with him and they had engaged all levels of service to deal with this. Despite all the clinical interventions that had been put in place, the smearing continued. The young person had been moved out of two placements because of the behavior and yet it continued. Reaching a point of total frustration, the adults started asking questions similar to the list above. Upon deeper investigation, they realized that the smearing only happened in the bathroom – not typical smearing behavior. It was place dependent and it seemed to also be time dependent – around the time the young person needed to use the bathroom. That took the focus away from the assumption that had been made – that the young person was doing it to express anger and seek attention. It turned out that the change in placements and diets were very different than what the youth was used to and it was a case of severe constipation that the young person was desperately trying to relieve. By thinking out of the box and questioning their assumptions, the young man's needs were met and the behavior stopped.

In the pages that follow, you will look, in detail, at six types of needs that many young people have that are not being met and strategies that can be considered to reimburse these needs. In the example you have just read, the young person had a biological need that, once understood, was easily reimbursed. The multiple theories that this NeuroTransactional model employs can be boiled down to two things:

1) We need to scan the child's ecology to see what they need to survive and survive well.
2) We need to plan to fill those gaps so that the young person gets what they need.

We believe that the brain and body, given positive relationships and experiences, have the ability to change negative experiences into positive outcomes. There is tremendous hope for all children and youth, no matter where they have come from, the experiences that they have endured, or the approaches they have used towards life.

Putting NeuroTransactional Practice into Action!

The model can be divided into two basic approaches: short-term or momentary management and long-term therapeutic planning (although as you can see below - the approaches are not mutually exclusive and can overlap or alternate between the two). For each approach there are options that therapeutic helpers can consider. In every challenging encounter that we have with our young people, the first thing we need to consider, and likely deal with, is the behavior in the moment. The key question at this point is; is this a "one-off" incident which when dealt with is done, or is this indicative of something that requires more in-depth planning? Either way, the first response is an appropriate NDI and if needed an ACT QUICK. Once the situation is under control, if the behavior is repetitive and self-defeating, more planning is required and we move to the long-term therapeutic planning approach. By asking a series of questions like the ones you see below, you can determine what basic needs are missing for the young person, and decide on one (or more) reimbursement(s).

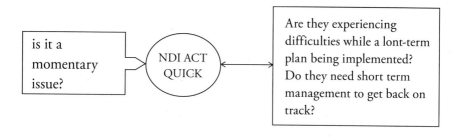

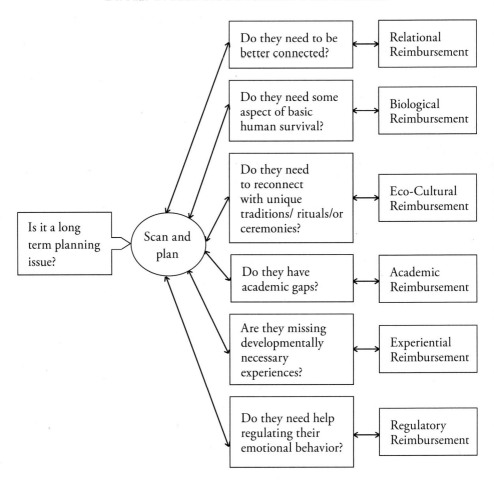

While some needs are quite apparent, without deeper reflection we may miss needs or not realize that one leads into another, and we may not properly reimburse that young person.

Story - Davis and the Diploma

Several years ago, a young man came into our program. He had been out of school for more than 6 months and was struggling to find a decent job without a high school diploma. He was strongly motivated and worked hard when he attended, but attendance was consistently a problem, as it had been at his local school before. One day when we were discussing the apparent contradiction between his desire to graduate and his attendance, he lost his temper and had a major melt-down. This was very unusual behavior and we needed to apply some "emotional first aid" and "ACT QUICK"ly to calm him and ask some more questions. With further investigation, we became aware that this young man was living under a bridge after having been kicked out of his home by his mom and step-dad. He was travelling many miles by foot to get to our program and living on whatever change he could make or beg. While academic reimbursement seemed like our initial choice, it quickly became apparent that biological reimbursements (shelter, food, and safety) took priority and needed to be addressed if anything else was to be accomplished successfully. Once we had dealt with those issues, we could then focus back on the academics. But it was a learning curve for all of us, and when he became overwhelmed or frustrated he would melt-down as he had never been taught or seen appropriate coping mechanisms (time for some regulatory reimbursement strategies) employed in stressful times. For months we needed to shift back and forth between short and long term approaches, often changing the reimbursements as required. Over time he learned that he could trust us, talk about how he felt when he was upset or stressed, and ask for help when he needed it and we learned to ask lots of questions, to keep asking them, and never assume. To be an effective therapeutic helper, it is vital that you can be flexible and go with the flow.

As you have just seen in the previous story, young people that you work with may require more than one type of reimbursement. In the sections that follow, you will see an explanation of each type of reimbursement followed by an example from actual programming, and possible strategies to consider. The purpose of the examples is to clarify and help define the parameters of that type of reimbursement. In all cases, it is safe to assume that more than one reimbursement was likely required and used but for clarity of explanation, we have described only the main one in each example.

In some cases, it is possible that there may be some overlap or "grey areas" when considering and labeling needs. For example, is a missing cultural experience considered to be an experiential reimbursement or an eco-cultural reimbursement? We would suggest that accuracy about the reimbursement itself is what matters - not the label (although just for the record, we would classify it as eco-cultural because of the culture component). Either way, as long as the young person has their needs met, the label becomes less important.

The Reimbursements

As a tiny, yet powerfully voiced young girl declared at a child welfare conference in South Africa, *"I am a child with problems, NOT a problem child!"* Our NeuroTransactional Model encourages caring individuals to "be with, feel with and go with" young people in need and see them as people with potential who simply need us to be a part of their lives. It involves therapeutically engineering specific reimbursements through new experiences found in the natural environment. We believe that the natural ecology provides the richest source of opportunity for realistic, positive change. Artificial environments are simply … artificial. The natural environment is defined in this model as the most independent environment in which a youth may safely live. We recognize that some youth will need unique levels of support or possibly supervision in specialized settings but, regardless of the setting, particular attention to the overall reimbursement plan must be considered if we are to help troubled youth with their developmental and relational needs. The reimbursement plan involves replacing what is developmentally or relationally owed to the child or youth in order to provide them with the necessary skills to function effectively in their environment and the flexibility to adjust to unfamiliar environments.

The Reimbursements are about supporting well-being. We identify six types of NeuroTransactional reimbursements: relational, biological, eco-cultural, academic, experiential, and regulatory. Although there are specifically six types of reimbursements presented in our model, the relational reimbursement will always serve as the foundational reimbursement needed to successfully transform youth. Without quality relationships with people, the brain becomes concerned for survival and will spend a significant amount of time trying to compensate. The personal experiences of the youth will have direct correlation to how well he or she can successfully compensate and to what degree reimbursement will be needed.

In all types of reimbursements the question to be asked is what particular aspects of reimbursement the youth needs and how they might be repaired. Repair in this model does not necessarily indicate that a problem must be completely solved. Rather, we feel that repair simply means to bring the youth to a better state that allows for more adaptive functioning and the opportunity to achieve his or her greatest potential. The act of repair must also consider who the key players would be in the reimbursement process. The goal in each of the reimbursements is to help youth "re-experience" missed opportunities through therapeutically engineered interactions and/ or supports. These interactions should always allow for maximum levels of independence and opportunities for input by the youth. However, many young people will require the therapeutic helper to "be with" them at a greater level. This higher level of being with them involves assisting youth with co-regulating their emotional states and providing them with more experiences that are therapeutically reimbursing. Simply put, new experiences that change the brain for the better must be provided.

Many youths with turbulent histories have dysregulated brain systems that are not yet equipped for the world around them. Therefore, therapeutic helpers must be able to help youth raise their levels of competence by modeling and providing "in the moment support" or proactive practice sessions. When youth see the therapeutic helper is competent and capable, their brains allow them to connect more deeply and the relationship is fortified and ripe for more intensive growth.

Social Emotional Learning and NeuroTransactional Reimbursements

In recent years, a greater amount of attention has been drawn to social emotional learning and its impact on academic success and positive social behavior (Durlak et al., 2011; Dymnicki, 2007). Core competencies across social emotional learning include: self-awareness, self-management, social awareness, relationship skills, and responsible decision-making. Our NeuroTransactional model enhances these competencies by expanding them further as reimbursements.

NeuroTransactional Reimbursement

Relationships are fundamental to therapeutic change. Paul Wachtel (2008) states that human beings exist in relationships. Our brain is a social brain that is constantly redesigning itself to survive. It recognizes when danger is looming or when safety is present. However, when environments change, the brain goes on alert and is extra vigilant to the activity around it. It is critical to remember that the brain has been shaped to survive. It does what experience has proven to be effective based on personal histories. This may mean the brain reacts impulsively or intentionally towards a person or thing within the ecology.

According to psychologists Miranda Lim and Larry Young (2006) relational interactions can be viewed as being composed of "four serial components: social recognition, social motivation, social approach, and social bonding" (p.31). When evidence leads the therapeutic helper to know that a youth's prior experiences connecting with people have been inadequate or missed completely and are in need of repair or replacement, a relational reimbursement is needed. Poor or non-existent relational attachments create an affective hunger and a desperate need for connection in both emotional and experiential ways. Long, Wood and Fecser (2001) believe that it is important to implement strategies that influence youth by using the strength of the relationship to convey approval of positive attributes "thereby strengthening confidence in themselves as valued people." They further state that this type of interaction "promotes qualities like helpfulness, fairness, kindness, leadership, and honesty" (p.57).

Young people who display oppositional behavior towards others have typically experienced aversive interactions with others who have responded to the youth through inconsistent, harsh, coercive, and generally ineffective strategies. Youth such as these often perceive themselves in negative ways and feel that they are "always in trouble" or that someone is always "mad at them." These perceptions breed internal frustration that eventually makes its way to the therapeutic helper as disturbing behavior. Youth express themselves by modeling the coercive, inconsistent ways of those they have known and fail to develop adaptive coping skills that resolve internal and external conflict in constructive ways. These maladaptive behaviors become entrenched and reinforced over time through similar dissatisfying relationships and interactions with peers and adults (Bugenthal, 1992).

Think back to the story of Krista. She had never really made a good enough connection with her parents. She felt neglected, ignored, and very much alone. New relationships are affected by the expectations developed in past relationships so while Krista wanted to connect, she was distrustful and assumed that all adults would ignore and neglect her. Through a series of trust trials, Krista and her teacher began to develop a relationship. Young people will often give us difficult situations that will sometimes be designed to drive us away, tempt us to become aggressive with them and trick us into believing that they are hopeless and lack the desire to succeed in life. We must never give up on any youth and strive constantly to find another "port of entry" when previous attempts have failed.

In many cases, troubled youth have not had sufficient logical experiences that have provided them with the necessary reasoning and predicting skills that might be needed to make wise decisions. This is true even with typical children and adolescent youth. Healthy adults, who are trained to recognize these needs of youth, must often step in to help them think things through and develop appropriate plans of action. The surrogate is temporary and steps away as soon as possible.

In some circumstances, youth find themselves in situations that require more than a surrogate brain interaction from an adult. These deeply intense and often dangerous situations often require trained adults to "jump in" and actually rescue the youth from themselves (e.g. suicidal ideation, suicidal attempts, homicidal thoughts). In times like these, youth are unable to see hope or predict positive outcomes for themselves and employ drastic measures that are risky or life threatening. Adults who are aware of these types of intentions are put into a mandated situation to seek help from qualified professionals. The act of rescuing youth from themselves actually is part of the trust trial interaction and ultimately fortifies the relationship and reimburses the youth with experiences that say that there are people in the world who do care and want him to be safe and alive.

NeuroTransactional Reimbursement Strategies

- Young people will assess you according to their experiences with other adults in your role. Your job is to re-craft their experiences by providing them with verbal and non-verbal affirmations that things "will be different here".

- Show them that you mean what you say by genuine and compassionate exchanges.

- Identify individual strengths in young people and use them for motivation and encouragement during tough moments.

- Allow the young people to guide interactions to promote a free flow of information even if, initially, you don't like that information. Let them show you that it is safe to be who they are. You can always sculpt gently later.

- Establish and encourage small opportunities for connection (micro-interactions). Not all pathways to connecting are long and involved. A quick hello or a "how is your day" shows that you care and that they are important.

- When the brain finds something humorous, the body responds in a positive manner both electrically and chemically. Use humor whenever it is appropriate. It is contagious and shifts emotions in a positive manner.

- Entering into relationships helps to create meaning for youth and therapeutic helpers. Making meaning helps us to link the present to the past and the future.

- Use helping relationships to open the door to a therapeutic opportunity and/or provide closure when needed. Therapeutic relationships can be instrumental in opening doors of hopefulness or closing doors of pain.

- Utilize multiple ports of entry to reach and teach challenging youth. If one approach does not work, try something else; and if that does not work, try something else. Never ever give up!

- Don't be afraid to negotiate. Trying to find a common ground helps us to see the pathway to get there.
- Peers are powerful. Use positive youth as tools for change.
- Use mentors. Therapeutic helpers can be transformative in the lives of young people. They can assist in the reimbursement of critical relational needs.

Biological Reimbursement - Basic Health and Safety Needs

For the most part, biological needs are the literal requirements for human survival. If these requirements are not met, the human body simply cannot continue to function. Air, water, and food are metabolic requirements for survival, the most basic need in Maslow's hierarchy. If these needs are not met they will take precedence over everything else and will dominate behavior. While the needs can be as basic as food, water, or shelter, they can also be pharmacological.

Story - Lisa and the Pills

Lisa came to the alternative program on her 13th birthday. She had been diagnosed as bi-polar at the age of nine, which is exceptionally young for a diagnosis of that kind to be made. Lisa had struggled in school, constantly running away and exhibiting inappropriate oppositional and sexualized behavior with staff and students, resulting in multiple suspensions. She lived with her mother, who suffered from several diagnosed mental health conditions as well. There were days when her teacher could make no inroads at all with Lisa and days where she was very compliant. Over time, it became apparent that Lisa's mother was not giving her the prescribed medications on a regular basis. Every time that Lisa exhibited appropriate behavior after a sustained period of medication compliance, her mother would see her as "better" and take her off the meds. It was not until Lisa cycled into a manic phase and caused trouble that her mother would put her back on her meds. This pattern continued for months as the teacher tried to get the mother to see the need to keep Lisa on her meds even when she was behaving appropriately. While Lisa likely needed other reimbursements as well, the primary reimbursement at the beginning of our time together was biological. She needed to take the medications prescribed by the psychiatrist before any other work could be done.

Biological reimbursements are not limited to medication. Anything needed to maintain basic body functions (like proper nutrition, adequate sleep, a roof over their heads, or proper clothing) will become a priority for disconnected young people. Keep in mind that according to Maslow's hierarchy of needs, if basic biological needs are not satisfied then these needs take priority in terms of focus and motivation.

Sleep is vitally important for the consolidation and reconsolidation of memories. While experiences or stimuli are encoded within milliseconds, the long-term maintenance of memories can take additional minutes, days, or even years to fully consolidate and become stable. Aspects of these memories are refined and remodeled during sleep. Verbal learning and cognitive performance are both negatively affected by sleep deprivation. Adequate sleep is required for optimal brain functioning and recent scientific evidence suggests that lack of sleep also inhibits the creation of new neurons or neurogenesis. A lack of sleep acts on the brain as a stressor resulting in the production of increased level of the stress hormone cortisol. High levels of cortisol inhibit neurogenesis in the hippocampus – the part of the brain necessary for the consolidation and refinement of memories. Adequate sleep is necessary for proper brain functioning, particularly in the classroom.

Biological Reimbursement Strategies

- Movement and exercise increase breathing and heart rate so that more blood flows to the brain, enhancing energy production and waste removal. Nearly half of young people ages 12 to 21 do not participate in vigorous physical activity on a regular basis. Provide opportunities to stretch or walk during the day. Incorporate physical activity into daily activities. Teach yoga or other relaxation strategies.

- Feed the brain for better learning. Adequate nutrition and hydration are necessary for optimal brain function.
- Mental and physical hygiene can take precedence over other needs. While hygiene can be a delicate issue, poor personal hygiene can lead to the feeling of being ostracized by peers and staff, lack of self-confidence, motivation, and increased susceptibility to illness.
- Disturbed sleep in young people affects their learning and various neurocognitive abilities negatively. Altering the start and finish times of the day, particularly for adolescents can assist with increasing the amount of sleep they get. Power naps for younger children can improve mood and learning.
- Forming an alliance with health care professionals can promote positive outcomes. Work together to encourage compliance.

Eco-Cultural Reimbursements - Unique Beliefs, Values, and Language

Eco-cultural reimbursement is honoring the fact that there are a variety of cultures and subcultures, as well as the differences within cultures that exist and need to be tapped into in order for a child or youth to feel safe and secure. When youth join new environments, their brains are constantly scanning for ways to connect socially in an attempt to survive well. All young people are unique individuals and their experiences, beliefs, values, and language affect their ways of interacting with others. Their brains are a result of their cultural experiences. It is the sights, sounds, tastes, people, ceremonies, and rituals that impact how they filter their world. "Ceremony and ritual give order, stability, and confidence to troubled children and adolescents, whose lives are often in considerable disarray" (Hobbs, 1994, p. 22). Respect for cultural distinctiveness is important to all young peoples' sense of self-worth and identity as well as their sense of belonging.

Prior to a therapeutic helper being able to respond in a culturally empathic and compassionate manner, it is imperative that they interact with each child or youth as a unique individual according to his or her own particular experiences. The culturally empathic therapeutic helper understands that the youth's experiences from another culture will always be different from theirs. The therapeutic helper must keep in mind how the personal experiences of the youth influence the experiences that they bring to the moment (Stewart, 1989).

When young people are moved from one place to another (be it from one foster placement to another, one country to another, one school to another school, or juvenile justice center to another juvenile justice center), they often experience either a loss of culture or a change in their cultural experience. For youth who have had little training in social skills, emotional flexibility, or positive support from others, these new experiences "rock the cultural boat" and will often cause them to be in a higher state of alert. When their culture has been restrained, altered, or lost, therapeutic helpers can help youth to understand the differences between their cultures and the new culture they are presently in. Therapeutic helpers should provide opportunities for them to reconnect with the traditions, rituals, and ceremonies unique to their own cultural past. It is also important for the therapeutic helpers working with youth from other cultures to have an understanding of how those cultures may have impacted their lives and how they filter their world here and now. Youth will always filter experiences through their cultural window, not ours.

The therapeutic helper wishing to provide eco-culturally relevant reimbursement will need to adjust, expand, or modify his or her understanding and methods of interacting with each child by considering the child's individual cultural history. To do this in a competent way, the therapeutic helper needs to increase his or her cultural awareness by opening a "cultural door." Not all ways of acting, thinking, feeling, or behaving will match those of the therapeutic helper. In fact, there will be many occasions when the youth will present behaviors that conflict culturally with those of the therapeutic helper. Programs need to adjust to the needs of the child. The child should not have to adjust to the needs of the program or the needs of the therapeutic helpers. Therapeutic helpers need to be sensitive to the needs and differences of these youth and be careful not to be judgmental or "make it all about their culture".

Relevant therapeutic helpers manage cultural influences as they surface, embracing them as part of the youth's revealing life story. By embracing these unique characteristics, the therapeutic helpers are better able to design suitable reimbursement experiences. Brendtro and Shabazian (2004) encourage adults to be aware of "major supports and stressors" in the child's environment that can empower the adult with important tools to help the youth. Even when external events are out of their immediate control or influence, adults can be powerful agents of change. They further stress that scanning the environment for the connections that already exist will allow us to gain a better perspective on the child's behaviors.

Story - Anan: I'll Get You Before You Get Me

Anan was a 16-year-old Sudanese refugee placed in a high school English as an additional language program. He had come to the country with his two older brothers after two years in a refugee camp. Life in the Sudan had been nothing less than horrendous. Militia showed up at night, abducting men and raping women. Some children were forced into labor; others, like Anan, witnessed their parents' murder. Life in the camps was not much better. He had never known any other way of life.

He had been referred to an alternative program after a suspension from school for carrying a concealed weapon. He had refused to cooperate with the administration upon the discovery of the weapon and became defiant and belligerent when the police were mentioned. He was deemed a safety risk and removed from the school for further assessment.

Anan had been teased and threatened by some of the students at the school. Historic trauma and distrustful thinking patterns based on evidence from his life in the Sudan had caused Anan to assume the worst and fear for his safety. One day when these particular students were taunting Anan, he had showed them the knife in an attempt to show that he was not afraid and would defend himself. This was immediately reported to the administration. Anan did not understand what he had done wrong and had defended his actions.

In this very complex situation, both Anan and the referring school required eco-cultural reimbursement. Anan needed help to see that while his life experiences had colored his views on safety and authority, not every country treated its citizens in the manner he had been treated; and that personal safety was a right so he did not have to defend himself. The school needed a better understanding of how Anan's ecology and culture had made him feel that his actions were necessary and find resources to help him adjust to life outside the Sudan. When working with refugee students, particularly ones who have had traumatic experiences in their country of origin, we need to remember that they are their experiences. Therapeutic helpers who promote comfort in these youth will help prepare their brains to perceive the world in a more logical, non-threatening way.

Strategies for Eco-Cultural Reimbursements

- Be cognizant of the fact that each person brings their own culture into all social interactions. Culture is personal – not exclusively unique to skin color, language, religious beliefs, or political affiliation.
- Once we are aware of cultural differences, therapeutic helpers should respect the specific rituals and ceremonies (cultural or religious) wherever possible.
- Values are transferred through people. Don't get hung up on your personal values.
- Keep in mind that change takes time. The brain can take extended periods to process the ecology of the new culture. Often we expect young people to adapt to a new ecology almost instantaneously. Give kids time. Their brains need that.
- Reflect critically on your own belief systems and values. You need to know yourself before you can accept the differences of others.
- Don't assume that simply telling a child or youth "this is how it is" will change their perception of the ecology. Familial, cultural, and peer viewpoints can have an overriding impact on their perceptions.
- Young people who have come from traumatic or tumultuous ecologies require special attention. Their emotional and social

well-being may supersede their ability to accept the new ecology. They need to feel that their ecology is stable, manageable, and understandable.

Academic Reimbursements - Educational Gaps

For many challenging young people, school experiences have either been intermittent or extremely negative. They may have academic gaps created by sporadic attendance or have come to see school and teachers as an additional source of stress and possibly threat. Life becomes shaped by reactivation of these memories, and they become the reality of present experience. School and teachers are often not good things in their lives. While negative emotions from threat and stress inhibit learning, arousal and positive emotions contribute significantly to attention, perception, memory, and problem solving.

Academic reimbursements can take many forms. If the youth are missing key literacy, numeracy, or content skills, programming can be provided to fill those gaps. If negative experiences are the problem, the establishment of positive, non-threatening learning environments can create opportunities for these young people to realize that success at school is a real possibility. In a positive school and classroom climate, all students feel physically safe and emotionally secure. They feel they have a sense of control, have sufficient time to learn, and the ability to deal with or get assistance dealing with their stress. In this climate, they are more likely to be successful and interested in learning. It is important to be mindful of the fact that most disconnected youth in schools are not just disconnected with their academic work, but disconnected with people. Their survival systems are in a state of hyperarousal, ready to strike at any moment and at the least little event.

In far too many instances, educational models fail to address the importance of re-connecting youth with people so that they feel safer to try new things, take appropriate risks, and pursue challenges more frequently. Increased interpersonal opportunities that result in success will undoubtedly promote greater self-esteem. However, if the student perceives a person called "teacher," "counselor," or "principal" as negative based on their personal history, relational reimbursement must take place first, or together with the academic reimbursement. People will always be the driving force behind transformation.

Story – Cindy: I'm Not Stupid!

It was a chilly March day when Cindy arrived at the off-campus program, dressed from head to toe in black. She was a very angry eighth grade student who came from a self-contained behavior classroom in a local middle school. When her teacher asked why she had been sent to the program, she replied, laughing, that she scared her regular middle school teachers. Her teacher asked her to elaborate and she said that she "freaked out" a lot and one day grabbed a caster from the bottom of the teacher's chair in the classroom and threw it at the vice principal's head. She added, remorsefully, that she had missed. Cindy was asked why (a question that does not get asked enough) she had thrown it at him and her story poured out. She said the behavior classroom teacher and that vice principal treated her like she was stupid. They talked down to her and they gave her single syllable words in spelling and basic arithmetic that "any five-year-old could do." She quite proudly informed her teacher she was a behavior problem and not a "retard." Sensing that even suggesting she tackle regular curriculum would be met with resistance, she was asked her what interested her. The answer was anime (a style of Japanese comic book and video cartoon animation in which the main characters have large doe-like eyes) and computers, so that was where they started. Since her new teacher knew nothing about anime, she was asked to tell her more about it. She chatted for quite a while. Her teacher asked her if she was familiar with PowerPoint. She was. Her first job then was to create a PowerPoint presentation on an anime show with character sketches for each of the main characters, the plot and setting of the story, and episodic summaries of each show in the series she had chosen. The work was well above grade level. She spent the rest of the year with her new teacher, challenging and completing all her seventh and eighth grade core academic subject courses and exams. She registered at the local high school for the fall with a different view of school and teachers and a different view of herself.

In Cindy's case, she needed an academic environment that was positive and non-threatening so that she could see that school was a place where she could be successful. Stress negatively impacts learning. Since the brain's priority is always survival, threat throws the brain into survival mode at the expense of developing higher-order thinking skills. If a classroom climate is negative, students will develop anxiety about the situation and feel stress. The endorphins that are released in low-threat environment are now replaced by cortisol affecting both high-order processing and memory consolidation.

Much like Krista, Cindy's experiences allowed her to change her perception of what a person called "teacher" meant. Her memories were also changed forever, and because of this experience she would no longer be able to say, or believe, that all teachers were "bad." Positive interactions with educational therapeutic helpers will also create and strengthen new, healthy neural pathways. These interactions will improve the way she will interact with and interpret her world.

Neurobiologists have known for a long time that a novel environment sparks exploration and learning. The "novelty center" of the brain, the substantia nigra/ventral tegmental area (SN/VTA), has a major impact on learning because it is linked to both the hippocampus (the learning center that consolidates learning memories) and the amygdala (the center for processing emotional information). They also know that the SN/VTA not only responds to novelty but that the novelty motivates the brain to explore the novel environment. The greater the novelty, the greater the desire to explore and learn more. This concept is beautifully demonstrated in the movie *Dead Poets Society*. In one scene you follow the students starting a new year at Welton private school. Teacher after teacher uses traditional teaching methods until the students meet their new English teacher, played by Robin Williams. His teaching methods are unorthodox by Welton standards. He whistles the *1812 Overture* while taking them out of the classroom to the hallway where old boy pictures are hung to focus on the idea of "carpe diem". He tells the students that if they feel daring they may call him "O Captain! My Captain!" (a reference to a Walt Whitman poem). The silence is palpable as every student is engaged and learning in their novel environment. Since the brain is built to ignore the old and focus on the new, any academic reimbursement will be more successful if novelty is involved.

Academic Reimbursement Strategies

- Many young people have had sporadic attendance in school and will have gaps in their education. Measuring existing strengths and weaknesses will help teachers start where the student left off and avoid frustration and low motivation when too difficult material is presented.
- Plan strategically in order to reach the needs of diverse learners in the classrooms today.
- Use learning strengths in the design and presentation of academic instruction. Include multi-sensory planning for auditory, visual, and kinesthetic learners. This ensures that enriched brain systems are maximized in the learning process.
- Evaluate students in traditional and non-traditional ways to ensure a more authentic assessment of abilities. Non-traditional forms of assessment ask students to perform real-world tasks that demonstrate meaningful application of essential knowledge and skills instead of relying on pen and paper assessments.
- Use novelty and humor wherever possible to capture the attention of the logical brain and increase motivation. Use the power of storytelling to help students learn. It helps the brain to make meaning of the bits and pieces from their own lives.
- Traditional instruction in schools is frequently left brain oriented. Instruction needs to be balanced to encourage the use of both hemispheres.
- Model the value-based behavior that you want to see in the classroom. The youth's mirror neurons are studying what you do, filing it away for future reference and use in similar circumstances.
- Young people ultimately determine what is interesting and motivating to them. As therapeutic helpers, we can only guess.

Innovative teachers are always looking for the smallest of sparks in the eye.

- Utilize culturally relevant education that capitalizes on success, flexibility, and self-determination whenever possible.

Experiential Reimbursements - Missing Developmental Life Experiences

From the first moments of life, the brain relies on human experience to learn. We are constantly drawn to interact with others. Experiences teach us what we should or should not do, helps us make decisions, and assist us in handling life's situations. They can change how we feel and teach us new things. They shape who we are and who we will become. To really understand something, you need to experience it.

Many of the young people we work with have not had the benefit of many of life's positive experiences. Fortunately, experiential reimbursements are often one of the easiest to repair or replace. Experiential reimbursement involves providing needy youth with developmentally necessary opportunities that would typically have been given to children within the same cultural environment.

It is easy for therapeutic helpers to become discouraged when certain social skills are not demonstrated by challenging youth. It is important to remember that experiences are everything in one's life. If a youth has not experienced typical events or had typical positive relationships, he or she will be at a significant disadvantage engaging in daily routines such as eating at restaurants, interacting with other drivers on the road, accepting compliments for good deeds, using the correct silverware during a formal dining experience, etc. In many cases, due to the lack of enriched experience, youth will either avoid these opportunities altogether or approach them with what limited skills they possess. Most youth try very hard to adapt and cope with new experiences, but without a fundamental base of social knowledge, they will struggle. True learning can only be gained from actual experience or approximating the experience. That is when therapeutic helpers play a significant role.

Neural pathways are developed and modified by life experiences and continue to change throughout the life span. Pathways that get attention and reinforcement through life experiences are kept and those that do not are eliminated. In addition, the life experiences creating and reinforcing the neural pathways need to be repetitive and occur over a span of time. The brain begins to see patterns in sights, sounds, and movements. The brain begins to build a framework of neural pathways that help us to process the information we are experiencing. The more we experience something, the stronger the pathways will be. As neural pathways are reinforced through experience, they serve as the foundation upon which all new information is interpreted making us able to negotiate similar but different experiences and make sense of our world.

Story – Shannon: The "Field Trip"

Shannon had been working in the alternative program for several months and had often mentioned that she really wanted to get a part-time job. She had gone to the local mall and picked up a handful of applications to fill in and her teacher had been working with her on her portfolio and cover letters. Shannon had had initial success with one application in particular and was called for a second interview downtown. All of a sudden her excitement turned to negativity. She said she wasn't going; she didn't want that stupid job anyway and gave the teacher a litany of excuses. Nothing rang true and her teacher questioned her further. She burst into tears. She had to take a bus to get there and she had never taken a bus and never been downtown. It was field trip time. With her teacher she learned how to access the bus times and routes on the computer and figured out how much it cost. They honed some map skills, finding the location downtown and then located the landmark buildings nearby. Her teacher drove the route for her, showing her where these buildings were as she followed on her map, and then they went for their "inaugural trip" and a dry run on the bus. The day of the interview she went alone, armed with a map, the address of the interview, and her cell phone in case something went awry and she needed the teacher. She made the trip, got the job, and didn't need to call her teacher's cell. She did however, get off at the wrong stop on the way home in her excitement, and was able to laugh it off when she finally showed up at the program, quite a bit later than expected because now she was an "experienced" bus rider and these things happened!

In Shannon's case, her positive, repetitive experiences over time with riding the bus allowed neural pathways to be laid down and strengthened. As the weeks passed and Shannon continued to be exposed to all the stimuli associated with riding the bus, her brain began to recognize patterns. She not only began to make sense of the physical part of taking the bus but also began to create a personal reality of what taking the bus looked like for her. The more she took the bus, the easier it became as her neural pathways were strengthened and the more confident she became. Taking the bus was now something that was no longer scary and something that she believed that she was capable of doing.

We are a result of our experiences that are made of both good and bad memories. Psychological health results from navigating a wide range of experiences successfully and from a balance between good and bad. We need just enough of each since too much of one or the other causes dysregulation in our brains and lives. The ability to successfully or unsuccessfully navigate these experiences shapes who we are and will become. Time is precious with dysregulated children. They need therapeutic helpers in their life as soon as possible to recreate relationships and experiences in order to retrain the brain into more positive, adaptive, and functional ways. The most important thing to remember is that people are the key to this transformation.

Experiential Reimbursement Strategies

- Understanding the youth's life story is critical. This assists us in identifying the youth's experiential strengths and needs. Without it, we have no reimbursement "road map".
- Use identified experiential strengths in seeking opportunities that reinforce self-esteem, self-concept, and self-efficacy.
- Identify typical developmental experiences that have been missed in their lives so that we may be with them, feel with them, and

go with them in a way that provides them with the skills and confidence necessary to be successful in life.

- Positive experiences as well as negative experiences are critical in shaping balanced brains. Teaching adaptive skills in good times and bad prepares the youth's brain for potential life challenges.
- Interactions need to be relationally genuine, in a language that they understand, and occur across the natural environment. This will increase the brain's receptivity and willingness to learn.
- Experiential reimbursements do not have to be complex. Simple interactions can oftentimes be the most transformative.

Regulatory Reimbursement - Self-Control and Appropriate Emotional Expression

The ability to regulate one's emotional behavior is critical. The amount of personal control we have over what we say, think, or do will determine how well we travel through life. Since emotions are built upon genetic and experiential aspects, we should keep these factors in mind when attempting to understand the "why" behind the behaviors our young people demonstrate as signs of their emotional states. We must then begin to teach them more effective ways of regulating themselves when faced with stress or challenge. Without such protective factors, young people will most likely respond in impulsive ways. Impulsivity or reactivity to life will undoubtedly lead to significant coping challenges. According to Daniel Siegel (1999) the ability to appropriately control our emotions is the "essence of self-regulation" (p.278).

During the early years of life, caregivers serve as our biggest regulators and usually undertake the majority of regulation for the child. As we develop, a natural desire to become more independent surfaces. Self-control, or the ability to regulate oneself, will depend on the structure, routine and experiences that have been historically shared by, and between, the caregivers and youth. If the caregiver provides sufficient stability, nurturance and co-regulation, the youth will be better prepared with skills to cope with the natural ups and downs of life. The positive experiences of coping well will inevitably become a part of the mental coping system and ultimately will be imprinted in the memory system as "a tool that worked." When correct tools prove to be beneficial over time and under a variety of circumstances, the tool will be added to the youth's mental toolbox for use in future interactions. This concept becomes important when therapeutic helpers are attempting to understand misbehavior. Linda Lantieri and Daniel Goleman (2008) explain that it is common for adults to mistake "unmanaged stress in our children as (intentional) inappropriate behavior that needs to be stopped." Lantieri and Goleman go on to say that youth are frequently "reprimanded for actions that are really stress reactions, rather than intentional behavior" (p.12).

John Arden (2010) states that as experiences accumulate within the brain, we develop neural pathways of routines that we will draw upon to make what is commonly called a "snap" decision. Spindle cells, found in large quantities within the cingulate cortex, assist us in making these types of decisions by connecting all the bits and pieces of prior experiences together quickly and efficiently. Spindle cells also aid in our ability to maintain attention and self-control and provide a unique interface between our thoughts and emotions. Spindle cells can only work with what they have to pull from within the brain's experiential file cabinet. For spindle cells to work in the best interest of the youth, the youth must first have experiences that are successful and socially proven.

Story: Frankie and the "Cigarettes"

Frankie had been a student in the alternative program for just over a year. He was not as mature as his counterparts and his behavior tended to set him apart. He struggled trying to fit in and seemed to have a tough time making and keeping friends. Staff members noticed that he was constantly trying to connect with other students, but these connections seemed to be short-lived. Students would tease him with their usual banter and Frankie would either get extremely angry and essentially throw a temper tantrum or go home in tears. This behavior led to further teasing and angry moments.

The staff was also concerned about the students he was connecting with. Inevitably, he seemed to be attracted to the students who often found themselves constantly "meeting" with the administration. One day a staff member noticed students smoking behind the school, a spot that was not designated as a smoking area. When the students were approached, it was apparent that they had not been smoking tobacco and they were brought to the office. They informed the staff that Frankie had supplied the green leafy matter they had been smoking. Frankie initially denied any involvement, screaming and swearing, trying to be tough like his "friends." However, a quick locker search confirmed the story and the cussing quickly changed to tears. He eventually told the staff involved that it was the only way those kids would be his friends.

The ability to regulate enables the self to alter its behaviors, increasing the degree that behavior is flexible and able to adapt. This flexibility allows youth to adjust to societal and situational demands that they encounter on a daily basis. In addition, the regulatory process prevents impulsive behavior that could be costly to the individual in the long-run, even when the short-term benefits are very great. Frankie was in need of regulatory reimbursement. Lacking the experience in connecting properly with others and an understanding of what true friendship actually entailed, Frankie was willing to do whatever it took to make a friend. Having friends mattered more than the potential consequences of his actions and he let his impulsive behavior get him into serious trouble. The staff realized that working with Frankie to help him develop and practice regulatory skills in a group setting was needed now.

If insufficient transactions and experiences have occurred, the youth will still attempt to seek maximum independence but will be insufficiently prepared to initiate and maintain appropriate self-regulation. This is when the trouble begins and direct conflict with the immediate culture becomes most apparent. Relationships become difficult to establish and maintain. The youth either travels through life independently doing the best that he or she can under the circumstances, or seeks out artificial attachments that have similarly poor levels of self-control to gain a sense of belonging. Traveling in a group for survival purposes is instinctual, but the selection of which group to travel in is a choice. Without the significant presence of positive caregivers and therapeutic helpers, youth can easily be drawn by and enchanted with negative novelty, further compounding their already challenged life. Providing regulatory reimbursement provides assistance to brain areas like the prefrontal cortex, amygdala, and hippocampus that are most responsive to learning and experiential transformation.

Regulatory Reimbursement Strategies

- Self-regulation is always preferred. At times, therapeutic helpers may need to assist a youth by co-regulating with him or her during moments of unbearable stress. Co-regulation should be temporary and last just long enough to jump-start the youth's safe and positive thinking. The helper should then back away and allow for maximum independence, jumping in only as needed.

- Model self-control and self-regulation in your words and actions when you are frustrated or under stress.

- Provide structure and predictability. The more freedom and flexibility they have, the more likely they are to give in to their impulsivity. Brains need stability and predictability in life. Healthy structure and routine are important as they instill safety and security. However, stability and predictability are reinforced when random moments of novelty or surprise are introduced.

- Impulses must be regulated. Youth must know when, where and how to approach life. Acting too quickly can have devastating effects. Teaching insight helps to inhibit neural pathways and can override primitive reactions.

- Provide a safe environment. Insight into thinking patterns assists in the right brain to right brain therapeutic exchange that is needed to retrain the brain and recreate pathways. This can only be done when the therapeutic helper and the youth feel safe and secure.

- Teach the skills of self-monitoring. It is necessary to keep track of behaviors in order to successfully self-regulate. Self-regulation results in increased attention and enhanced working memory, so youth will learn more in a shorter period.

Hope Through Compassion

Compassion involves genuine concern for those who are suffering or "at-risk" in life. When compassion is truly felt, there will be a natural motivation to help. Troubled youth do not grow from dependence to independence by themselves. Therapeutic helpers are needed along the way. Research in resilience has shown us that it only takes a single person to make a therapeutic difference in a troubled youth's life — a line we have heard time and again. Although it has been commonplace to hear such a statement, genuine therapeutic helpers actually embrace this belief and actualize it when working with troubled young people, radiating true compassion with every footstep taken, every word spoken, and every sound heard.

As therapeutic helpers demonstrate sensitive, caregiving responses to even the most challenging of behaviors by youth, there is a direct correlation with higher levels of positive emotional states, lower levels of negative affect, greater self-esteem, and increased social competence (Suess, Grossman, & Sroufe, 1992). Simply by "being with, feeling with, and going with" youth, therapeutic helpers begin to set the stage for hopeful transformation, fortifying individual strengths and empowering the brains of troubled youth for the journey called life.

Key Terms - Chapter 5

academic reimbursement	NeuroTransactional support
artificial attachment	regulatory reimbursement
biological reimbursement	reimbursement
eco-cultural reimbursement	relational reimbursement
experiential reimbursement	

References

Ainsworth, M., Blehar, M., Waters, E., and Wall, S. (1978). *Patterns of attachment.* Hillsdale, NJ: Erlbaum.

Alarcón, J. M., Malleret, G., Touzani, K., Vronskaya, S., Ishii, S., Kandel, E. R., & Barco, A. (2004). Chromatin acetylation, memory, and LTP are impaired in CBP+/- mice: A model for the cognitive deficit in Rubinstein-Taybi syndrome and its amelioration. *Neuron, 42,* 947–959.

Alvarez RP, Chen G, Bodurka J, Kaplan R, Grillon C. Phasic and sustained fear in humans elicits distinct patterns of brain activity. *Neuroimage* (2011) 55(1):389–400. doi: 10.1016/j.neuroimage.2010.11.057

American Psychiatric Association. (2000). *Diagnostic and statistical manual of mental disorders (4th ed., rev).* Washington, DC: Author.

Andreasen, N.C. (2005). *The creating brain: The neuroscience of genius.* Washington, DC: Danna Press.

Arden, J.B. (2010). *Rewire your brain.* Hoboken, NJ: John Wiley & Sons.

Baker, P.W. (2007). Neuroscience and the helping process. In N.J. Long, W.C. Morse, F.A. Fecser & R.G. Newman (Eds.). *Conflict in the classroom: Positive staff support for troubled students (6th ed.).* Austin, TX: Pro-Ed.

Baumeister, R. F., and Leary, M. R. (1995). The need to belong: desire for interpersonal attachments as a fundamental human motivation. *Psychol. Bull.* 117, 497–529.

Bernard, B. (2004). *Resiliency: What we have learned*. San Francisco, CA: WestEd.

Berridge, K.C., and Robinson, T.E. (1998). What is the role of dopamine in reward: Hedonic impact, reward learning, or incentive salience? *Brain Res. Brain Res. Rev.* 28, 309-369.

Bowly, J. (1969/1982). *Attachment and loss, vol 1: Attachment*. New York: Basic Books.

Bradenoch, B. (2008). *Being a brain-wise therapist: A practical guide to interpersonal neurobiology*. New York: Norton.

Brendtro, L., & Shabazian, M. (2004). *Troubled children and youth: Turning problems into opportunities*. Champaign, Illinois: Research Press.

Bromberg-Martin, E.S., Matsumoto, M., & Hikosaka, O. (2010). Dopamine in Motivational Control: Rewarding, Aversive, and Alerting. *Neuron*: 68 (5), 815-

Bronfenbrenner, U. (1979). *The ecology of human development*. Cambridge, MA: Harvard University Press.

Brown, J., Cohen, P., Johnson, J. & Salzinger, S. (1998). A longitudinal analysis of risk factors for child maltreatment: Findings of a 17 year prospective study of official recorded and self-reported child abuse and neglect. *Child Abuse and Neglect, 22*, 1065-1078.

Bugenthal, D.B. (1992). Affective and cognitive processes within threat-oriented family systems. In I.E. Sigel, A. McGillicuddy-de Lisi, & JJ. Goodnow (Eds.). *Parental belief systems: The psychological consequences for children* (2nd ed., pp.219-248). Hillsdale, NJ: Erlbaum.

Carter, C.S. (1998). Neuroendocrine perspectives on social attachment and love. *Psychoneuroendocrinology*, 23, 779-818.

Cohen, J.A., Deblinger, E., Mannarino, A. P., & de Arellano, M. A. (2001). The importance of culture in treating abused and neglected children: An empirical review. *Child Maltreatment*, 6(2), 148-157.

Cozolino, L. (2006). *The neuroscience of human relationships*. New York: WW Norton & Co, Inc.

Csikszentmihalyi, M. (1990). *Flow: The psychology of optimal experience*. New York: Harper and Row.

Damasio, A. (1994). *Descartes' error: Emotion, reason, and the human brain*. New York: Norton.

Damasio, A. (2003). *Looking for Spinoza: Joy, sorrow, and the feeling brain*. New York: Norton.

Daw, N.D., Shohamy, D. (2008). The Cognitive Neuroscience of Motivation and Learning. *Social Cognition, 26 (1)*. 593 - 620.

Devinsky, O. (2000). Right cerebral hemisphere dominance for a sense of corporeal and emotional self. *Epilepsy and Behavior. 1*, 60-73.

Diamond M. C., 1988 *Enriching Heredity*, The Free Press, New York.

Diamond M. C., Krech D., Rosenzweig M. R. 1964 *The effects of an Enriched Environment on the Rat Cerebral Cortex*. Journal of Comparative Neurology, 123,111-119.

DeKoven Fishbane, M. (2012). Neurobiology and family processes. In Froma Walsh (Ed.), *Normal family processes: Growing diversity and complexity*. (pp. 553-574). New York, NY: Guildford Press.

Doidge, N. (2007). *The brain that changes itself*. New York: Penguin Books.

Durlak, J. A., Weissberg, R. P., Dymnicki, A. B., Taylor, R. D., & Schellinger, K. B. (2011). The impact of enhancing students' social and emotional learning: A meta-analysis of school-based universal interventions. *Child Development*, 82, 405-432.

Dymnicki, A. (2007). *The impact of school-based social and emotional development programs on academic performance.* Chicago, IL: University of Illinois at Chicago.

Ekman, P. (1992). Facial expressions of emotions: New findings, new questions. *Psychological Science.* 3, 34-38.

Ekman, P. & Davidson, R. (1994). Affective science: A research agenda. In P. Ekman & R. Davidson (Eds.) *The nature of emotion: Fundamental questions.* New York: Oxford University Press. Pp.411-430.

Edelman, G.M. & Tononi G. (2000). *A universe of consciousness.* New York: Basic Books. (38)

Elizinga, B. & Roelofs, K. (2005). Cortisol-induced impairments of working memory requires acute sympathetic activation. *Behavioral Neuroscience, 119,* 98-103.

Fang, X., Brown, D. S., Florence, C. S., & Mercy, J. A. (2012). The economic burden of child maltreatment in the United States and implications for prevention. *Child Abuse & Neglec*t, 36(2), 156-165. http://dx.doi.org/10.1016/j.chiabu.2011.10.006.

Figley CR, ed. (1995). *Compassion Fatigue: Coping With Secondary Traumatic Stress Disorder in Those Who Treat the Traumatized.* New York: Brunner/Mazel.

Frankham, J., Edwards-Kerr, D., Humphrey, N. & Roberts, L. (2007) School exclusions: Learning partnerships outside mainstream education. York: Joseph Rowntree Foundation.

Garfat, T. (2008). The inter-personal in-between: An exploration of relational child and youth care practice. In G. Bellefeuille & F. Ricks

(Eds.), *Standing on the precipice: Inquiry into the creative potential of child and youth care practice*. Edmonton. AB: MacEwan Press.

Gilbert, L. K., Breiding, M. J., Merrick, M. T., Thompson, W. W., Ford, D. C., Dhingra, S. S., & Parks, S. E. (2010). Childhood adversity and adult chronic disease: An update from ten states and the District of Columbia. *American Journal of Preventive Medicine*, 48(3), 345–349. http://dx.doi.org/10.1016/j.amepre.2014.09.006.

Glauser, A.S. & Bozarth, J.D. (2001). Person centered counseling: The culture within. *Journal of Counseling and Development*, 79(2), 42-147.

Goleman, D. (2006). *Social intelligence*. New York: Bantam Dell.

Goleman, D. (1998). Working with emotional intelligence. New York: Bantam Books.

Grennough, W.T., Black, J.E. & Wallace, C.S. (1987). Experience and brain development. *Child Development*, 58, 539-559.

Hebb, D. O. (1949). *The organization of behavior*. New York: Wiley & Sons.

Hobbs, N. (1994). *The troubled and troubling child*. Cleveland, OH: American Re-Education Association.

Horgan, G. (2007). The impact of poverty on young children's experience of school. York: Joseph Rowntree Foundation.

Iacoboni, M. (2008). Mirroring people. New York: Farrar, Straus and Giroux.

Iacoboni, M., Koski, L.M., Brass, M., Bekkering, H., Woods, R.P., Dubeua, M. et al., (2001). Reafferent copies of imitated actions in the right superior temporal cortex. *Proceedings of the National Academy of Sciences, USA*, 98, 13995-13999.

Jacobs, G.D. (2003). The ancestral mind: Reclaim the power. New York: Penguin Books.

Johnson, Steven (2004). *Mind wide open: Your brain and the neuroscience of everyday life.* New York, NY: Scribner.

Kagawa-Singer, M. & Chung, R. (1994). A paradigm for culturally-based care in ethnic minority populations. *Journal of Community Psychology, 22*(2), 192-208.

Kawamoto T, Ura M, & Nittono H (2015) Intrapersonal and interpersonal processes of social exclusion. *Front. Neurosci.* 9:62.

Kellett, M. & Dar, A. (2007). *Children researching links between poverty and literacy.* York: Joseph Rowntree Foundation.

Kitayama, S., & Park, J. (2010). Cultural neuroscience of the self: Understanding the social grounding of the brain. *Scan* 5, 111-129.

Knight LK and Depue BE (2019) New frontiers in anxiety research: The translational potential of the bed nucleus of the stria terminalis. *Front. Psychiatry* 10:510. doi: 10.3389/fpsyt.2019.00510

Kolb, D. A. (1984). *Experiential learning: Experience as the source of learning and development.* New Jersey: Prentice Hall.

Lantieri, L. & Goleman, D. (2008). *Building emotional intelligence: Techniques to cultivate inner strength in children.* Boulder, CO: Sounds True.

Lipina, S. J., & Colombo, J. A. (2009). *Human brain development series. Poverty and brain development during childhood: An approach from cognitive psychology and neuroscience.* Washington, DC, US: American Psychological Association.
http://dx.doi.org/10.1037/11879-000

Le Doux, J. E., (2015). *Anxious: Using the brain to understand and treat fear and anxiety*. New York: Penguin Books.

LeDoux, J.E. (1996). The emotional brain. New York: Simon and Schuster.

Long, N. J., Wood, M., & Fecser, F. A. (2001). *Advanced instruction in life space crisis intervention: The skill of reclaiming young people involved in self-defeating patterns of behavior*. Hagerstown, MD: Life Space Crisis Intervention Institute.

Lim, M.M. & Young, L.J. (2006). Neurology of the social brain; Lessons from animal models about social relationships. In S.R.H. Beach, M.Z. Wambolt, N.J.Kaslow et al. (Eds.),*Relational processes and DSM-IV: Neuroscience, assessment, prevention, and treatment*. Washington, DC: American Psychiatric Publishing.

Maslow, Abraham (1954). *Motivation and personality*. New York: Harper.

Matsumoto, D. (1996). *Culture and psychology*. New York: Brooks/Cole Publishing.

McGowan P.O., Sasaki A, D'alessio A.C., Dymov S, Labonte B, Szyf M, Turecki G, Meaney M.J. (2009) Epigenetic regulation of the glucocorticoid receptor in human brain associates with childhood abuse. *Nature Neuroscience*.12:342–348.

Mehta D, Klengel T, Conneely KN, Smith AK, Altmann A, Pace TW, Rex-Haffner M, Loeschner A, Gonik M, Mercer KB, Bradley B, Müller-Myhsok B, Ressler KJ, Binder EB. (2013). Childhood maltreatment is associated with distinct genomic and epigenetic profiles in posttraumatic stress disorder. *Proceedings for the National Academy of Sciences,* 110(20):8302-7.

Mesquita, B. & Ellsworth, P.C. (2001). In K.Scherer, A. Schorr & T. Johnstone (Ed.) *Appraisal processes in emotion: Theory, methods, research* (pp.233-247). New York: Oxford University Press.

Miller, G. E., Chen, E. & Zjou, E. S. (2007). If it goes up, must it come down? Chronic stress and the hypothalamic-pituitary-adrenocortical axis in humans. *Psychological Bulletin, 133*, 24-45.

Mikaelsson, M.A., & Miller, C.A. (2011). The path to epigenetic treatment of memory disorders. *Neurobiology of Learning and Memory*, 96: 13-18.

Miller, J., Kahle, S., & Hastings, P. (2017). Moderate baseline vagal tone predicts greater prosociality in children. *Developmental Psychology* 53 (2), 274–289 © 2016 American Psychological Association.

Moore, T., McArthur, M., Roche, S., Death, J., & Tilbury, C. (2016). *Safe and sound: Exploring the safety of young people in residential care.* Melbourne: Institute of Child Protection Studies, Australian Catholic University. Royal Commission into Institutional Responses to Child Sexual Abuse, Sydney.

NCTSN Core Curriculum on Childhood Trauma Task Force (2012). *The 12 core concepts: Concepts for understanding traumatic stress responses in children and families.* Core Curriculum on Childhood Trauma. Los Angeles, CA, and Durham, NC: UCLA-Duke University National Center for Child Traumatic Stress.

Orth, U. (2018). The family environment in early childhood has a long-term effect on self-esteem: A longitudinal study from birth to age 27 years. *Journal of Personality and Social Psychology*, 114(4), 637-655.

Panksepp, J. (1998). *Affective neuroscience: The foundations of human and animal connections.* New York, NY: Oxford University Press.

Perry, B. (2009). Examining maltreatment through a neurodevelopmental lens: Clinical applications of the neurosequential model of therapeutics. *Journal of Loss and Trauma*, 14, 240-255.

Perry, B. (2006). Helping a traumatized child. *The Brown University Child and Adolescent Behavior Letter*, Apr 2006 Supplement, 22, 1-2.

Perry, B., Pollard, R. A., Blakely, T. L., Baker, W. L., & Vigilante, D. (1995). Childhood trauma, the neurobiology of adaptation, and "use-dependent" development of the brain: How "states" become "traits." *Infant Mental Health Journal, 16*(4), 271-291.

Pinker, S. (1997). *How the mind works.* London: Penguin Books.

Porges, S. W. (2011). *The Norton series on interpersonal neurobiology. The polyvagal theory: Neurophysiological foundations of emotions, attachment, communication, and self-regulation.* New York, NY, US: W W Norton & Co.

Porges, S. (2009). *The polyvagal theory: New insights into adaptive reactions of the autonomic nervous system.* Cleveland Clinic J. Med.76 (Suppl 2): S86–S90.

Porges, S. W., Doussard-Roosevelt, J. A., & Maita, A. K. (1994). Vagal tone and the physiological regulation of emotion. *Monographs of the Society for Research in Child Development, 59*(2-3), 167-186, 250-283.

Prilleltensky, I. (2018, February 27). *The context of well-being.* IPPA Positive Psychology Leaders Series

Powell, Kendall. "How does the teenage brain work?" *Nature.* August 2006.

Ratey, J, (2001). *The user's guide to the brain.* New York: Random House.

Restack, R. (2006). The naked brain: How the emerging neurosociety is changing how we live, work and love. New York, NY: Harmony.

Roer-Strier, D. (2001). Reducing risk for children in changing cultural contexts: Recommendations for intervention and training. *Child Abuse & Neglect, 25*(2), 231-248.

Rogers, Carl. (1951). *Client-centered therapy.* Boston: Houghton Mifflin.

Roseman, I.J. (1984). Cognitive determinants of emotion: A structural theory. In P. Shaver (Ed.). *Review of personality and social psychology: Vol. 5 Emotions, relationships, and health* (pp.11-36). Beverly Hills, CA: Sage.

Roth, T.L., & Sweatt, J.D. (2009). Regulation of chromatin structure in memory formation. *Current Opinion in Neurobiology*, 19: 336-342

Sapolsky, R. M. (2004). *Why zebras don't get ulcers.* New York: Henry Holt and Company.

Sapolsky, R. M., Romero, L. M., & Munck, A. U. (2000). How do glucocorticoids influence stress responses? Integrating permissive, suppressive, stimulatory, and preparative actions. *Endocrine Review. 21,* 55-89.

Scherer, K.R. (2000). Emotional expression: A royal road for the study of behavior control. In A. Grob & W. Perrig (Eds.*), Control of human behavior, mental processes, and awareness* (pp.227-294). Hillsdale, NJ: Erlbaum.

Schore, A. N. (2003). *Affect regulation and disorders of the self.* New York: W.W. Norton and Company.

Schore, A. N. (2003). *Affect regulation and the repair of the self.* New York: W.W. Norton and Company.

Schore, A. N. (2000). Attachment and regulation of the right brain. *Attachment and human development, 2,* 23-47.

Schore, A.N. (1994). *Affect regulation and the origin of the self: The neurobiology of emotional development.* Hllsdale, NJ: Erlbaum.

Sharot, T., Ricardi, A.M., Raio,C.M., & Phelps,E.A. (2007). Neural mechanisms mediating optimism bias. Nature. 450, 102-105.

Siegel, D. (2010). *Mindsight: The new science of personal transformation.* New York: Bantam/Random House.

Siegel, D. (2007). *The mindful brain: Reflection and attunement in the cultivation of well-being.* New York, NY; Norton.

Siegel, D. (2001). Toward an interpersonal neurobiology of the developing mind: Attachment relationships, "mindsight" and neural integration. *Infant Mental Health Journal, 22*(1-2), 67-94.

Siegel, D. (1999). *The developing mind: How relationships and the brain interact to shape who we are.* New York, NY; The Guilford Press.

Singer, T. & Klimecki, O.M. (2014). Empathy and Compassion. *Current Biology,* 24, 875-878.

Smith, R.J. and Steindler, E.M. (1983). The impact of difficult patients upon treaters. *Bulletin of the Meninger Clinic,* 47(20), 107-116.

Springer, M.V., McIntosh, A.R., Wincour, C., & Grady, C.L. (2005). The relation between brain activity during memory tasks and years of education in young and older adults. *Neuropsychology, 19*(2), 181-192.

Stewart, I. (1989). Transactional analysis counseling in action. London: Sage.

Stien, P. T. & Kendall, J. (2004). *Psychological trauma and the developing brain: Neurologically based interventions for challenging children.* New York: Routledge.

Stillman, T. F. & Baumeister, R. F., (2009) Uncertainty, belongingness, and four needs for meaning. *Psychological Inquiry,* 20:4, 249-251.

Suess, G.J., Grossman, K.E., & Sroufe, L.A. (1992). Effects of attachment to mother and father on quality of adaptation: From dyadic to individual organization of self. *International Journal of Behavioral Development,15,* 43-65.

Sutton, L., Smith, N., Dearden, C. & Middleton, S. (2007). *A child's-eye view of social difference.* York: Joseph Rowntree Foundation.

Van der Kolk, B. (1996). The body keeps score: Memory and the evolving psychobiology of posttraumatic stress. *Harvard Review of Psychiatry,1,* 253-265.

Weaver I., Meaney M.J., Szyf M. (2006). *Maternal care effects on the hippocampal transcriptome and anxiety-mediated behaviors in the offspring that are reversible in adulthood.* Proceedings of the National Academy of Sciences. 103:3480–3485.

Wexler, B. E. (2006). *Brain and culture: Neurobiology, ideology, and social change.* Cambridge, MA; Massachusetts Institute of Technology Press.

Wachtel, P.L. (2008). *Relational theory and the practice of psychotherapy.* New York, NY: Guilford Press.

Yellow Horse Brave Heart, Maria (1999). Oyate Ptayela: Rebuilding the Lakota Nation through addressing historical trauma among Lakota parents. *Journal of Human Behavior and the Social Environment* 2(1/2): 109-126.

Zull, J. E. (2002). *The art of the changing brain: Enriching teaching by exploring the biology of learning.* Sterling, VA: Stylus.

For Further Information and/or Training Contact:

www.thepersonbrain.com

About the Authors

Paul W Baker, Ph.D is a developmental neuropsychologist who has worked with troubled children and youth for over twenty years. He currently resides in Atlanta, Georgia, USA and Newcastle,NSW, Australia. He has direct experience in working with troubled youth as a special education teacher, school administrator, clinical administrator, psychologist, foster parent and adoptive parent. Dr. Baker is the developer of The PersonBrain Model™, a strength-based training program for working with challenging youth. The model incorporates brain-based strategies that are practical, effective and supportive of youth. Dr. Baker provides brain-based consultative services to schools, child and youth care facilities, juvenile justice programs, residential facilities, and professional groups. Paul is a regular contributor to professional development in the field of neuroscience and youth work and is a frequent speaker at international conferences. He may be contacted at paul.baker@personbrain.com

Meredith White-McMahon, Ed.D is a veteran educator of at-risk children and youth. She has been teaching for 33 years at all levels K-12. and currently lives in Winnipeg, Manitoba. Dr. White-McMahon has contributed to the development of numerous scientific writings and textbooks currently used in the university setting. In 2011 she co-authored The Hopeful Brain: Relational Repair for Disconnected Children and Youth that incorporates brain-based strategies that are practical, effective and supportive of youth. Her experience as an educator has earned her wide respect for innovative and positive supports in the transformation of challenging youth. Dr. White-McMahon is a Senior Trainer of The PersonBrain Model™ providing training to a wide audience. She also provides training and consultation services in crisis intervention and relational areas such as attachment, trauma, attention, depression, anxiety, and oppositional-defiance. She can be contacted at Doctriplem@gmail.com